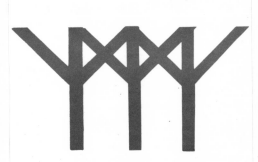

Civic Garden Centre
Library

A
PLANTSMAN'S GUIDE TO
LILIES

M. JEFFERSON-BROWN

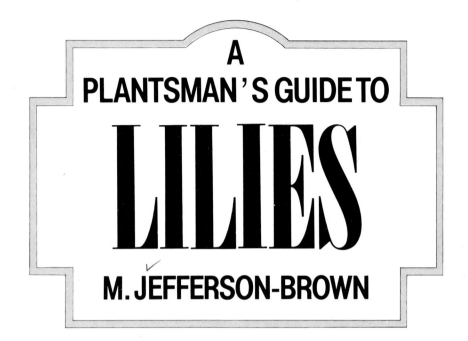

A
PLANTSMAN'S GUIDE TO
LILIES

M. JEFFERSON-BROWN

SERIES EDITOR
ALAN TOOGOOD

WARD LOCK LIMITED · LONDON

First published in Great Britain in 1989
by Ward Lock Limited, 8 Clifford Street
London W1X 1RB, an Egmont Company

House editor Denis Ingram

Text filmset in Times
by Dorchester Typesetting Group Ltd.
Printed and bound in Great Britain by
Hazel Watson & Viney Ltd
Member of the BPCC Group,
Aylesbury, Bucks.

British Library Cataloguing in Publication Data

Jefferson-Brown, Michael, *1930-*
    A plantsman's guide to lilies
    1. Gardens. Lilies. Cultivation
    I. Title   II. Series
    635.9′34324

ISBN 0-7063-6753-7

CONTENTS

PUBLISHER'S NOTE

Readers are requested to note that in order to make the
text intelligible in both hemispheres, plant flowering
times, etc. are described in terms of seasons, not
months. The following table provides an approximate
'translation' of seasons into months for the two
hemispheres.

Northern Hemisphere		Southern Hemisphere
Mid-winter	= January	= Mid-summer
Late winter	= February	= Late summer
Early spring	= March	= Early autumn
Mid-spring	= April	= Mid-autumn
Late spring	= May	= Late autumn
Early summer	= June	= Early winter
Mid-summer	= July	= Mid-winter
Late summer	= August	= Late winter
Early autumn	= September	= Early spring
Mid-autumn	= October	= Mid-spring
Late autumn	= November	= Late spring
Early winter	= December	= Early summer

Captions for colour photographs on chapter opening pages:

Pp. 8-9 Valued for its early blooms, *L. pyrenaicum* is strong
and adventurous enough to escape through the garden gate
into the wild.

Pp. 20-21 The Madonna lily, *L. candidum*, cultivated for
over 2,000 years, looks well in a cottage garden or other
traditional setting. Site it clear of other lilies to keep it
healthy.

Pp. 36-37 Stalwart *Lilium henryi*, growing 2.5 m (8 ft) or
more high, is among the easiest of lilies on all soils.

Pp. 56-57 'Destiny' was one of the new hybrid lilies bred in
Oregon and introduced as Mid-Century Hybrids in the
1950s.

Pp. 76-77 This large showy Asiatic with outward-facing
flowers is 'King Pete'.

Pp. 104-5 'Bright Star' is the most successful of its type,
derived from interbreeding trumpets with *L. henryi*. These
hybrids were formerly known as Aurelians.

Pp. 120-1 The wonderful snow-white Oriental group hybrid
'Casablanca' looks breathtaking in pots or in acid soil
between dark-leaved rhododendrons.

EDITOR'S FOREWORD

This unique series takes a completely fresh look at the most popular garden and greenhouse plants.

Written by a team of leading specialists, yet suitable for novice and more experienced gardeners alike, the series considers modern uses of the plants, including refreshing ideas for combining them with other garden or greenhouse plants. This should appeal to the more general gardener who, unlike the specialist, does not want to devote a large part of the garden to a particular plant. Many of the planting schemes and modern uses are beautifully illustrated in colour.

The extensive A-Z lists describe in great detail hundreds of the best varieties and species available today.

For the historically-minded, each book opens with a brief history of the subject up to the present day and, as

appropriate, looks at the developments by plant breeders.

The books cover all you need to know about growing and propagating. The former embraces such aspects as suitable sites and soils, planting methods, all-year-round care and how to combat pests, diseases and disorders.

Propagation includes raising plants from seeds and by vegetative means, as appropriate.

For each subject there is a society (sometimes more than one), full details of which round off each book.

The plants that make up this series are very popular and examples can be found in many gardens. However, it is hoped that these books will encourage gardeners to try some of the better, or perhaps more unusual, varieties; ensure some stunning plant associations; and result in the plants being grown well.

Alan Toogood

CHAPTER ONE

PAST AND PRESENT

Lilies need no gilding: few plants produce such beauty in such diversity and with such an ever-fresh appeal. Some lily admirers are fanatical; it becomes an all-consuming passion; they give up cricket, stamp collecting, drink and ·. . . well lots of things to follow their obsession. Others, constrained by the need to earn·a living and to maintain marital harmony, spend·what time they can with their lilies; other plants have to wait their turn. Some lack the courage to pursue their love, since nothing so lovely can be easily cultivated; its beauty is too daunting.

Do not hesitate. If you have not tried lilies or have only attempted a few, do try planting some.

There are about seventy species of *Lilium* growing in the wild. They are scattered around the world in the Northern Hemisphere. One group is native to North America; other groups straddle Europe and the Russian land mass; many grow in Asia, their first point of origin, especially in China and Japan, while others grow in the highlands of Burma and India and one or two descend into the Indian mainland. They can be found growing by the seashore, or at considerable altitudes. Sometimes a species hailing from some exotic spot might be thought an unlikely plant for temperate climates. What may be forgotten is that the bulb's habitat in its sun-blest foreign home may be at a considerable altitude and cooler than a glance at a map might suggest.

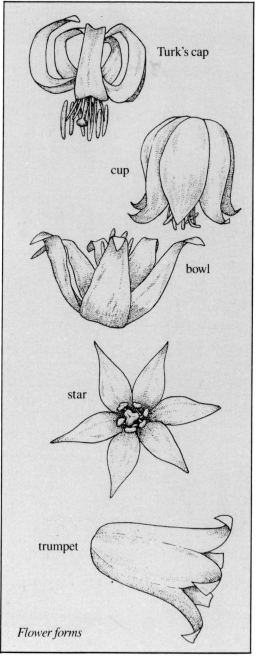

Flower forms

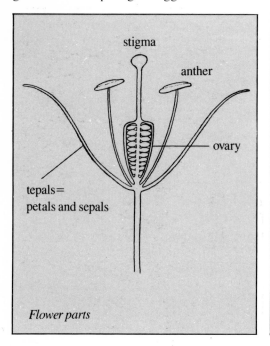

Flower parts

Bulbs are of various forms, but all have independent loose scales not completely enclosing the growing point as do those of daffodils and tulips. This can make them a little more liable to damage when out of the ground, but the scales offer an easy means of propagation and so this slight inconvenience can be turned to advantage. Growth above ground outside is made throughout spring and is rapid. From late spring until autumn is well advanced, there need not be a week without lilies in bloom. Plants may range from only about 15cm (6in) high to giants that outreach the tallest man in the kingdom. Flower sizes range from 2–3cm (1in) to over 30cm (1ft) across. Colours include white, yellow, orange, red, pink, mauve and many combinations. Many are high-ly perfumed. There are some difficult species to test the skills and patience of gardeners; there are many wildlings and hybrids that are child's play.

Having amazed us with their flowers, the plants begin to die back. Pods may begin to swell and eventually be found full of flat disc-like seeds, maybe well over a hundred in a pod. Going forth and multiplying is done with energy and diversity by the lily. Apart from seed, the scales may be broken from the bulb and induced to form small bulbs. Stems of many kinds either carry bulbils naturally in their leaf axils or may be persuaded to do so. The bulbs themselves will divide, some with greater abandon than others. On the stem below ground there may be several young bulbs clustering. Some few kinds have

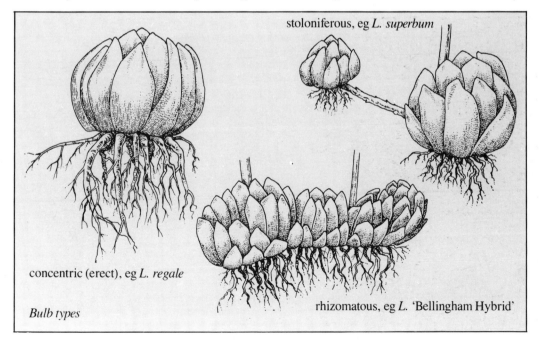

stoloniferous, eg *L. superbum*

concentric (erect), eg *L. regale*

rhizomatous, eg *L.* 'Bellingham Hybrid'

Bulb types

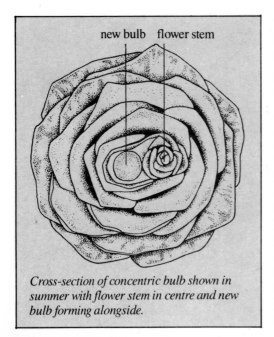

new bulb   flower stem

Cross-section of concentric bulb shown in summer with flower stem in centre and new bulb forming alongside.

wandering stems under the soil surface that produce bulbs at intervals en route, all of which is very satisfying.

IN THE PAST

A few lilies have been grown in Britain for many centuries. The martagon lily is one that has occasionally jumped over the garden wall and gone native. Yellow-flowered *L. pyrenaicum* has done the same thing in one or two spots in the south, but it is *L. candidum*, the Madonna lily, that has had the longest history of cultivation in Europe. It was early associated with Christianity and often featured in religious paintings and carvings. In many ways it is an unusual lily, not least of its idiosyncracies being that it flourishes better in a cottage

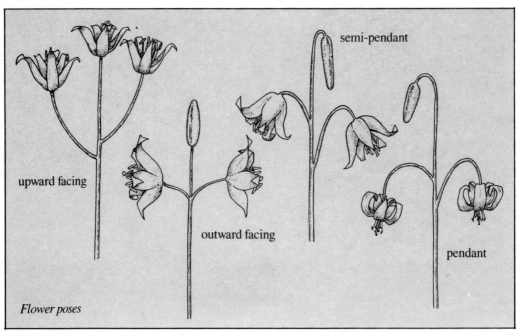

upward facing

outward facing

semi-pendant

pendant

Flower poses

Long known in cultivation, L. canadense is one of the most distinctive of the American group of species.

garden than under the hand of the acknowledged lily buff. This is the only lily of which we have cultural records in medieval Britain.

John Gerard listed three European kinds in 1596, *L. martagon, bulbiferum croceum,* and *chalcedonicum.* As early as 1629, *L. canadense* had crossed the Atlantic to tease gardeners with its beauty and difficulty. A few more were added at intervals through the 1700s and then in the 1880s the riches of the East were added, culminating in the intro-duction of the fantastic *L. auratum* in 1862. Curiously it was only in 1904 that the first bulbs of that wonderful garden lily, *L. regale,* first arrived in Europe. This prodigy took to cultivation splen-didly. There was no shortage of stock. Very freely produced seeds could be grown into plants that bloomed in their second season, without fail in their third.

Partly due to the very good reputation soon gained by *L. regale,* interest in lilies has increased steadily through this century. The introduction of many easy-to-grow hybrids has revolutionized the gardener's concept of the lily from the 1950s onwards.

WILD LILIES

Lilies evolved from primitive kinds in Asia. Closest to the envisaged ancestor type is the species *L. hansonii,* native to eastern Russia and a Japanese island. Botanists point to certain characteristics as being primitive in this genus; the simple entire bulb, the upright stem, leaves arranged at stages in whorls like the spokes of a cartwheel, the recurved petals, and the orange-yellow colouring. From such an original species may have developed *L. martagon* which then spread across Russia into the Balkans and Europe. Derived from the same original species, a plant may have crossed the land link into America and established the closely related group of species there, many of which are found in the mountain ranges that sweep down the west side of the land mass. *L. martagon* and most of the American species have in common the distinctive whorled foliage, and recurved petals.

In Asia, some plants would have broken from the whorled foliage pattern fairly early on and have scattered leaves up the stems. In some can be detected a spiral pattern. They could have been plants of *L. lancifolium (L. tigrinum)* type. At the same time one or more strong plants like *L. dauricum* may have developed to become *L. dauricum* in the East and *L. bulbiferum* in the West, in Europe.

Size and form of flowers became more diverse, the curled up so-called 'turkscaps' being augmented by bowl-shaped starry ones and others with funnelled trumpets more or less opening at the mouth.

Below ground things were happening too. The original round normal shaped concentric bulb like that of 'Enchant-ment' or *L. regale* was mixing with other enterprising kinds, forming stolons, long underground stems from the bulb, with new bulbs forming at their ends. In America some species adopted a dif-ferent approach; *L. pardalinum* kinds formed bulbous mats with growing points shown by gathered scales: rhizomatous bulbs. Some went only halfway along this road, keeping a more or less normal concentric bulb but lurching sideways with new growth, so called sub-rhizomatous bulbs. One or two Asian species produced shoots from bulbs that instead of making straight for the surface wandered sideways before growing into the air. This bit of lily lateral thinking had the benefit of producing one, two or three bulbs on the subterranean wandering stem.

Lilies are a diverse lot. There is no end to their fascination and no lily grower pretends to know more than a part of the truth about this most interesting genus. There is always something to learn.

Lilies are now on the march. They have taken up almost permanent occupation in every florist's premises throughout the year, and can also be found in garden centres, chain stores, and the corner hardware shop. We purchase their flowers in millions.

In the past the lily was often bracketed with orchids as a rich man's hobby. Professional gardeners might know the secret of growing them but they were thought to be difficult; beautiful of course, but capricious. Happily much has changed: prices of many bulbs are very reasonable and new hybrids are easy to grow. Attractive pictures in catalogues and showcases are not unrealistic fantasies. Lilies can be for everyone.

Lilies can be grown in gardens large and small, with or without lime in the soil, and may even be grown in all sorts

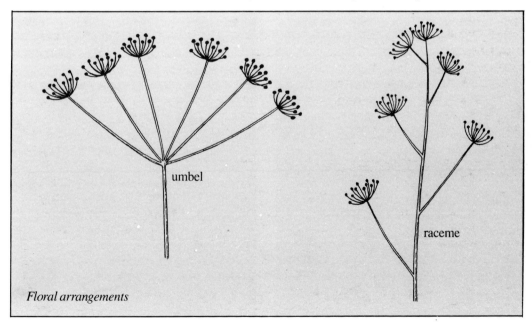

umbel

raceme

Floral arrangements

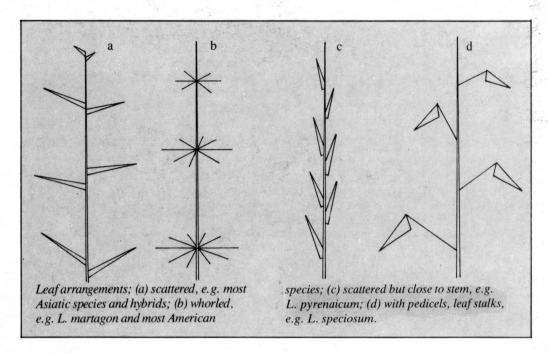

Leaf arrangements; (a) scattered, e.g. most Asiatic species and hybrids; (b) whorled, e.g. L. martagon and most American species; (c) scattered but close to stem, e.g. L. pyrenaicum; (d) with pedicels, leaf stalks, e.g. L. speciosum.

of containers without any garden at all. In stately home, suburban garden, or city patio the lily is bringing colour, excitement and magic. Large numbers are grown in pots, and it is a constant surprise to rediscover how quickly and easily they manage in such containers, easier by far than daffodils, tulips and hyacinths, the traditional bulbs for pots.

MODERN LILIES

It is little wonder that growers were soon attracted to the idea of hybridizing lilies. This has happened worldwide. Early work in Holland and Britain was probably predated by the Japanese working with their native kinds. Various enthusiasts in Europe, Canada and America were joined by others in Aus-

tralia, New Zealand and Russia. All were beguiled by the beauty of the flowers. Sometimes the desire to establish the relationships of species was the starting point. More often there was just the wish to try for new colours and shapes.

Much fine work was done by many individuals, often in quite small gardens. However, the present popular boom in hybrid lilies is due in a very major part to the work of one individual. Jan de Graaff working in Oregon had the dutch background of bulb culture to draw on as well as the Dutch orderly business sense. This was

Opposite: Lilium martagon, a charming species that has been cultivated for centuries, is easy on most soils and naturalizes well.

combined with the American attitude that all things are possible and that new is likely to be better. He assembled a team of dedicated people and started a monumental programme of lily hybridization. He collected species from all parts of the world as well as all the current hybrids. The best forms of the species were sought out and improved by careful selection of generations of seedlings.

While lots of hybridization programmes were undertaken, two had almost immediate impact on gardens worldwide. One programme aimed to raise early-flowering races of flowers of mixed parentage from such Asiatic species as *L. davidii*, *L. lancifolium* and *L. dauricum*, together with the European *L. bulbiferum* and hybrids grown under various names such as L.× *hollandicum*, L.× *umbellatum* and L.× *maculatum*. These were first launched as Mid-Century Hybrids and included the irrepressible 'Enchantment'. The second major programme was the breeding of new trumpets. These were of greater vigour than those previously grown and covered a vastly wider colour range.

'Enchantment' and all its relatives belong to a group of hybrids called Asiatics. Despite the exotic sounding group name, they are easy plants. Apart from this ease of culture they are characterized by rarely being above 1 m (3 ft) high, having many wide-open flowers, being in bloom in early and mid-summer, and having no or very little scent. The trumpet series are plants that can grow from 90 cm–2 m (3–7 ft) high, can have half a dozen to over 30 large trumpet-shaped flowers, and have very powerful perfumes. They tend to bloom later, in mid and late summer.

In New Zealand, America and elsewhere such miracles as *L. auratum* and *L. speciosum* have long tempted breeders. New hybrids of these lovely late blooming kinds are constantly being raised. The flowers make orchids look passé, and apart from their almost unbelievable appearance, they are worth growing for their scent alone. One can almost get intoxicated by it.

The fundamental point about the modern lily is that it is so very easy to propagate commercially (a new kind can be into tens of thousands very quickly) and so they can become quickly available. Raising new kinds is not difficult. You could have a go and find yourself the breeder of a new 'Enchantment' ready to conquer the world.

THE FUTURE

Of all ornamental plants it would be difficult to choose one of which we could say so surely that 'its time has come'. It fits beautifully into the technology of mass production under glass, and it can be grown well in the open. It is a hardy plant that the modern gardener with limited space can accommodate easily between his shrubs and plants. It makes the most splendid of pot plants in bloom fourteen weeks from planting. It may be grown to perfection by someone with only a small patio or by the owner of half a county.

The diversity of colour, form, size, habit and character make a lifetime too short a period to study the lily. The fact that there are some wild species that are frankly difficult in cultivation means that there is always a challenge waiting for the gardener who is not happy except when trying to succeed where most fail. Happily most are easy if their basic wants are met.

Hybridizing is an easy matter technically, though there are problems with the crossing of some kinds, their genetic make-up inhibiting some matings. Pollen grains applied to the sticky stigma grow rapidly down to fertilize the many egg cells waiting to make a potential podful of seed. Pods may have a hundred to two hundred viable seeds. You do not need many flowers to start a substantial programme of breeding. As most of the popular kinds have seed that can grow into flowering bulbs in very short periods, perhaps a couple of seasons, it will be realized that this is a hobby that could appeal to many. In the past some of the most successful breeders have only had modest gardens.

There is room for a series of very early lilies, ones that bloom in May and early June like *L. pyrenaicum*, in a variety of colours. Is it an impossible dream to think that maybe some time in the future breeders will manage to produce flowers of mixed *L. speciosum* and *L. auratum* ancestry but which are tolerant of lime so that we can all plant them outside in the garden and not have to be content with them growing in pots? New species are being introduced into the hybrid series bred between *L. martagon* and *L. hansonii*, stalwart lime tolerant kinds, and so there is a definite possibility of greater variety amongst these. The new series of North hybrids from *L. lankongense* are scented, unlike the others of the Asiatic group. It would be lovely to have the 'Enchantments' and 'Sterling Stars' of the lily world having not only looks but a scent as well. Such dreams are close to gilding the lily!

CHAPTER TWO

PLANTING IDEAS

While lilies are brilliant plants on their
own, they like to grow in association
with other plants as they do in the wild.
Contrasting shrubs, trees, herbaceous
plants, ferns and other garden inhabi-
tants enhance the lily's beauty and
character. Flowers add colour and drama with a touch of exotic magic. Quiet
corners of the garden become sites for
pilgrimage when lilies bloom. Just a
few bulbs can transform their sur-
roundings into a lively focal point,
where garden visitors are carefully
propelled, gin and tonic in hand. They
stop to look. 'Oh yes. I popped in a few
bulbs a couple of years ago. Almost
forgot about them. Quite nice aren't
they?'

PLANT ASSOCIATIONS

The fact of the matter is that the lily is a social plant. It enjoys the company of neighbours to shade its root run. Like clematis, the rule is 'head in the sun and toes in the shade'. Of course, balance has to be maintained; the shrubs that cast their shade cannot be allowed to stifle the lilies, but this maintenance of balance and order is what gardening is all about. Most of us like to get the framework of the garden built and then enjoy tinkering and gently improving the design, but spend most time enjoying and tending the plants.

Lilies we enjoy because, apart from their beauty, they are ever fresh. The complete antithesis of a cactus that looks the same year after year, the lily in growth is always on the move. Fat buds burst through the soil, stems lengthen daily, flower buds appear and swell and open in succession. The first flower is followed in many kinds by a dozen or two dozen more, while in some there may be up to a hundred flowers on a single stem. There's value for you! Even after flowering the stems are not without beauty. The seed pods are impressive and take on most lovely shapes, some reminiscent of elegant Greek urns.

Some wild species not only welcome the shade provided by neighbours but are pleased to have the support of shrubs. *L. davidii willmottiae* with dozens of dark spotted orange turkscap flowers has arching stems that need stakes or shrubby support to hold their brilliant loads aloft. Useful shrubs for this supporting role include lavender and rosemary.

As elsewhere in the garden some of the most pleasing of plant associations work because of their contrasting colours, shapes, sizes, textures and habits. The upright stems of lilies with clean-cut foliage are enhanced by their opposites. A clump of broad-leaved hostas at ground level forms a complete contrast. They grow and expand as the lilies grow. *Sedum maximum*, with grey-green succulent leaves, is another distinctive herbaceous companion.

Others can be less successful. A stand of *Lilium martagon* naturalized with a backing of shrubs and trees in my own garden has been invaded by foxgloves.

Lilium martagon in grass; one of the best naturalizing species.

These are normally welcome guests, free to colonize where they will, but they bloom at the same time as the lilies, with tall spires of flowers often of similar colouring. So they diminish rather than enhance each other's beauty. Around my lilies they have to be considered weeds.

Other shrubs, besides the lavender and rosemary I've mentioned, that make good companions for lilies include the smaller berberis, evergreen and deciduous. They form a complete contrast to the lilies' habit. Some spiraeas, such as *S. arguta*, are equally useful – small-leaved and fresh, with attractive flowers early on, but tidied away before the lilies take all eyes.

PERMANENTLY PLANTED LILIES

Some lilies are planted permanently as one might position a shrub or tree. Bulbs of *L. pardalinum*, *L. p. giganteum* and other American types will be allocated a site on a very long lease. They will be there for decades, each season expanding their colony size. Their neighbours need choosing with care. Rampaging forsythias, philadelphus or deutzias are big bold extrovert plants so need to be planted at some distance. More circumspect rhododendrons might be a possibility. Lilies and rhododendrons form a traditional partnership: the shrubs give shelter, support, background colour and contrast to the lilies. As most of these enjoy somewhat acid soils like rhododendrons it is a natural alliance.

Fanciers to be cast away on a desert island and allowed only one lily are likely to be torn between *L. speciosum* and *L. auratum*, both plants of great character. *L. speciosum* with quite broad-stalked leaves pointing outwards cuts patterns into space. The gracefully hanging flowers with broad swept-back petals may be a lovely crimson pink, with darker spots, but there are all variations from pure white to more or less uniform crimson. Wiry stems carry a wide pyramid of blossom beautifully spaced. *L. auratum* is a complete miracle. Its flowers form huge stars, each wide white petal having a central stripe of gold and often flushed or even heavily painted crimson so that many are tricolored, white, gold and red or pink. As flowers can be 30cm (1ft) across and stems can carry many blooms, it would provide solace and wonder on that desert island. Of all lilies, these of the Oriental Group are the most strict lime haters. A whiff of lime and they begin to curl up. This makes them natural actors in the gardens where rhododendrons flourish. As the lilies bloom towards the end of summer, this is a happy partnership. Lilies come into their own when the rhododendrons are flowerless.

Martagon lilies and their hybrid races are kinds that one expects to last for a century or so, if not forever, increasing in number as bulbs divide but more especially as the masses of seeds produce seedlings that can colonize wide areas. There are gardens where martagons have been in residence well over a hundred years. They can transform light

Opposite: *Lilium pardalinum will grow happily for decades in most soils.*

woodland, a glade, or a shrub border, into a magic land when each stem hangs out dozens of their smallish curled up flowers. Species flowers can be shades of mauve-pink, ivory white, or aubergine maroon, colours that charm and have perhaps even greater long-term appeal than the more blatant oranges and reds of the 'Enchantment' fraternity. Hybrids with *L. hansonii*, like the Paisley or Backhouse Hybrids, may have these same colours but can be ambers, near tangerines, and interesting tan shades. Greater or lesser amounts of spotting add to the overall charm when one comes from a distance to inspect the flowers more closely.

Where a number of these grow together they create a haze of colour below or between shrubs or trees. In such a setting they look more natural and graceful. One does not need broad acres to create such a picture. Between a winter-flowering viburnum, with *Senecio greyi* to the fore and clumps of evergreen berberis behind, a few lilies can look captivating. Happily all the martagons and their hybrids will flourish in any soil – lime is no bar. Blooming in early summer they follow the spring display of many shrubs.

Where soil conditions preclude the growing of rhododendrons as lily companions, there are plenty of other shrubs ready to take on the role. Dark-leaved hazel, *Corylus maxima* 'Purpurea', will make a dramatic contrast. Some of the quick-growing hebes are shorter-growing. *Eucalyptus gunnii*, as a normal tree, or coppiced to produce a fountain of rounded silver-blue juvenile foliage, will make a stylish contrast of form and colour.

These strong-growing lilies will manage in rough grass and look well. Here one could also try a group of the dwarfer, sturdy, very early *L. pyrenaicum*. One begins to look for their yellow turkscaps in late spring. They are

□ PERMANENT LILIES: SHORT LIST

L. pyrenaicum	yellow	late spring–early summer
L. martagon	mauvey pink	early–mid summer
L. martagon album	ivory white	early–mid summer
L. martagon cattaniae	dark maroon	early–mid summer
L. hansonii	orange yellow	early–mid summer
L. Backhouse Hybrids		early–mid summer
L. Paisley Hybrids		early–mid summer
L. pardalinum	orange, crimson	mid summer
L. p. giganteum	gold, crimson	mid summer
L. 'Buttercup'	gold	mid summer
L. 'Cherrywood'	cherry red, gold	mid summer
L. Bullwood Hybrids		mid summer
L. Bellingham Hybrids		mid summer

to be viewed at a reasonable distance as they have an unfortunate odour. Their active pungency may delight visiting insects and encourage them in their pollinating duties: there is method in their malodour.

IN BEDS AND BORDERS

Asiatic Hybrids come with sturdy stems carrying flowers looking upwards, outwards or downwards, but are predominantly upward-facing like 'Enchantment'. What they lack in feminine grace they more than make good in easy manners, and bright, extrovert colours. Standing 60–90 cm (2–3 ft) high they are strong stakeless plants excellent in beds and borders. Brilliant in early and mid summer, they are as happy in the front as further back, but look best with accompanying plants, mixing well with shrubby things like lavender, rosemary, escallonia and hydrangea, or with herbaceous paeonies, lupins, ligularias, artemisias and ferns. Some of the best effects are with contrasting foliage.

Shiny whorled leaves and vertical ramrod stems of *L. pardalinum* or *L. martagon* contrast with the silky or hairy greys and silvers of artemisia, senecio and lavender. Broad-leaved hostas, variegated or plain, and the dark purple-green claw-edged leaves of ligularia can make the shiny willow-shaped leaves of Asiatic Hybrids look clean-cut and healthy.

The pure herbaceous border is now to be found only in a very few gardens. It used to lack interest and form in the long winter months and so in our smaller gardens it is an indulgence only tolerated if one spends the winters in the Caribbean and has someone willing to do all the work of lifting, splitting and replanting, while you enjoy the sun. As far as the lily is concerned the more modern vogue of a mixed border that takes in shrubs is wholly to be welcomed. Two things are a worry to the lily grower and a hazard to the plant: late spring frosts and searing cold winds just as the young growths are poking through the soil. Shrubby neighbours

---

□ **BED AND BORDER LILIES: SHORT LIST**

L. 'Sunray'	60–90 cm (24–30 in)	gold	early summer
L. Citronella Strain	90 cm–1.2 m (36–48 in)	lemon gold	early–mid summer
L. 'Harmony'	60 cm (24 in)	amber	early summer
L. 'Enchantment'	75 cm (30 in)	orange	early summer
L. 'Heritage'	90 cm (36 in)	orange	early summer
L. 'Corina'	75 cm (30 in)	pinky crimson	early–mid summer
L. 'Red Night'	75–90 cm (30–36 in)	dark red	early–mid summer
L. 'Rosita'	75–90 cm (30–36 in)	mauvey pink	early–mid summer
L. 'Zephyr'	75 cm (30 in)	pink	early–mid summer
L. 'Sterling Star'	75–90 cm (30–36 in)	white	mid summer
L. regale	75 cm–1.5 m (30–60 in)	white	mid–late summer
L. Trumpet Hybrids	90 cm–1.8 m (36–72 in)		mid–late summer

Lilies grow happily between shrubs that shade the soil and give shelter.

can temper the wind and deflect much of the damaging thrusts of frost.

The short list above is of the hardier and somewhat more extrovert types. They can look quite splendid in mixed borders and beds. However, the point is worth making that the lily is such a 'classy' plant, that some may argue it is best separated from the distraction of daisies, lupins, roses and the like. British class consciousness is an abomination, but perhaps in the garden things are different.

To do duty around and beneath our flowering lilies the less dominant brooms and gorses are excellent. They are a complete contrast and will shade the root run perfectly, while providing bright bloom early in the season, as well as some shelter and support.

Best company for our bulbs are totally dissimilar non-competitive plants, mainly shrubs, smaller ones to the fore and both small and larger ones to the rear. However, one type of plant completely different from the lilies can grow in association with them, each complementing the other. These are the hardy ferns. Many of them may not be much use as wind or frost protection early in the year, but they grow and expand with the lilies and, having no competing flowers, produce such very different foliage that the partnership works splendidly. This association is not unknown in the wild.

Ferns, in particular the hardy ones, have become a personal obsession. Their myriad forms and stylized beauty are more and more absorbing. Forms of

Dryopteris filix-mas (male fern), and *D. dilatata* (broad buckler fern) have intricate proper fern-like fronds that are more or less evergreen and so make somewhat more ideal companions than the slightly lighter, more graceful deciduous *Athyrium filix-femina* (lady fern), a hugely diverse species. Be careful about starting with ferns, for, as collections, they are addictive. Over three hundred forms of the lady fern alone have been named. *Osmunda regalis*, the large royal fern, might be used behind a group of lilies, but it is a big one and can spread 3 m (10 ft) across.

Another range of companions that go well with lilies and ferns are the grasses. They vary from tiny tufts of thin wispy leaves to the large fountains of Pampas. Some intermediate ones, having done their annual turn, die back to attractive winter colours of russet, fawn, brown and pale shades. In spring new growth appears. With many, this will be relatively late, and they thus provide support for the young shoots of over-wintering lilies. The foliage of the many grasses is diverse; all are different from those of the lilies and could be complementary. Some of the variegated ones might add a lighter touch to the whole ensemble.

THE LILY BORDER

A lily border may once have been recommended without reservation. Now restraints of space and experience have taught us that it is a mistake to keep all our golden eggs in one basket. Alas, in this world, all creation is subject to the perils of natural competi-
tion, and viruses can reduce some lilies to ruin. Viral infection is spread mainly by sap-sucking insects like aphids. Shrubs between our clumps of lilies cannot stop aphids completely but they do provide surprisingly effective barriers that deter many.

THE WILD GARDEN

Fashions change in gardening as elsewhere. Sometimes changes are dictated by economic necessity, sometimes by the availability of plant material, sometimes by a change of mood, or occasionally as the result of some new or revitalized tenet of gardening lore. At present the idea of a wild garden is very popular.

The need to conserve our wild flowers has led to countless packets of wild flower seeds being sold. People may think that a wild garden may not need much tending. This is not so. Management of turf containing cowslips, primroses, fritillaries, orchids and a miscellany of other characters is going to need careful thought and work. It is merely a different form of husbandry.

Aiming for a natural undisciplined appearance can be achieved on different scales depending on the size of garden. In spring we aim to have sweeps of snowdrops, wild daffodils, bluebells and wood anemones, together with primroses and cowslips. Later we are happy to see the bedstraws, the mallows, all forms of wild geraniums, including the

Opposite: *Lilium szovitsianum grows well and will colonize in a wild garden.*

meadow cranesbills, harebells, wild aquilegias and ragged robin.

Some lilies will do well here. Start with the early-flowering *L. pyrenaicum* with its yellow curled-up flowers; follow these with the many forms of martagons and their hybrids. Try *L. szovitsianum* with wide bowl-shaped trumpets of sulphur-yellow and dream of the hillsides in Georgia which are turned yellow with its blooms. Strong American species like the *L. pardalinum* types will do especially well in moist spots where many others would fail. Though subject to virus and perhaps banned as a possible health hazard and carrier of dreaded diseases, late-flowering tiger lilies can extend the season, and if you raised some from seed you may be sure of starting with clean stock.

Hybrid lilies are not the thing for the wild garden. We want to aim for a more natural look. Lilies we choose for this part of the garden have to be stayers. Life is real and life is earnest.

HANDLING COLOUR

Some Asiatic Hybrids are so aggressively bright that they need siting with care: a clump of 'Enchantment' can kill other colours around. It is certainly worth growing, being early, so vivid and easy. Perhaps it is best in a bold group near the garden entrance with rich-leaved evergreen shrubs as a backing. Yellow can be quite dominant too; we welcome the daffodils in the spring. In early summer the sun will light up 'Connecticut King', 'Sunray' and many other cheerful lilies. The strong blues of simple flowers like forget-me-nots or love-in-a-mist can surround the yellow lilies and make a pleasing picture. The ferny foliage of nigella is a particularly good contrast to the lily's boldness.

Other Asiatics are less domineering with pale creams and whites, such as 'Medaillon', 'Mont Blanc' and 'Sterling Star', which merge with almost any colour. However, they are not insipid, and their clear-cut starry flowers will not clash with rhododendrons, poppies or lupins.

Having spent a lifetime growing, breeding and selling daffodils as well as lilies, I have enjoyed rich colours, but always it is the cooler shades, the lemons, the creams and pastel shades that I have found most acceptable in my own garden. Indeed, I now tend to plant more herbaceous things that have pink, mauve, white and cream flowers than the brighter reds and golds. I would not be without the more vivid lilies, but they need to be used sparingly if a restful atmosphere is sought. Of course, a few clumps accentuate the value of the cooler shades.

Asiatic Hybrids with *L. cernuum* blood may be pinky mauve and have narrow dark leaves. Others like 'Rosita' are pleasing; the dark stems and foliage as well as the pinky stars look especially well when associated with silver- or grey-leaved plants.

A new race of lilies bred from *L. lankongense* by Dr North rings the changes. Many of them are named after members of the North family. These are much more graceful flowers, wiry strong stems carrying pyramids of pendant flowers with recurving petals in many pastel shades. Each cultivar is often a medley of soft mingling colours, ivories, buffs, pinks and mauves, with darker spotting. They are a most bewitching race. They bloom in mid rather than early summer and will be decorative for several weeks. The open graceful demeanour of the blooms makes them ideal in a herbaceous border or between shrubs of almost any kind. They stand a bit taller than most of the 'Enchantment' types, at 90 cm–1.2 m (3–4 ft).

As a generalization the American group species have flowers of orange and gold. They tend to bloom in mid summer. Once they have been found a spot where they are happy they are probably best left alone to grow, flower and increase. The strongest of the Americans will grow in almost any soil. I have had them flourishing in very heavy clay, but the trickier ones need good drainage, especially through the winter months. They need a lot of water during the months of active growth, but prefer to be kept fairly dry through the winter. At home they may be tucked under deep snow. These considerations must be taken into account when planting the bulbs. Shrubs and trees help to provide natural drainage by penetrating and helping to form the structure of the soil.

Commonest garden kinds of the American group are *L. pardalinum* and *L. giganteum*, together with the related Bellingham Hybrids. These are all unfussy strong-growing kinds with upright stems, stylized whorled foliage and nodding flowers with recurved petals.

Usually they are rich gold with their petal ends touched with bright scarlet and all are liberally sprinkled with very dark spots. As they bloom at a time when there are relatively few flowering trees and shrubs, the place for groups of these may well be between such plants. This is not to say that they need to be banished from borders or beds. They can look dramatic as taller clumps among lower growing heucheras, artemisias, true geraniums, hostas and pyrethrums. We may have lupins making a higher point, or spikes of delphiniums, and further away may be macleaya. Lily foliage looks fresh and exciting, in the same way as that of paeonies, and, out of bloom, this foliage can still be pleasing in its own right. American species colours are usually bright and account should be taken of this. If you want drama in mid summer but cannot manage bright uniformed lilies in your border, then the softer coloured trumpets may be better. *L. regale* has much to commend it. It is easy, prolific in bulb and flower, has splendid purple buds, looks magnificent with its final wide white golden-throated trumpets and overflows with all the perfume of the Orient.

THE NUMBERS GAME

Garden spectacles are not made from niggardly plantings. The Romans knew all about spectacles. Post-Roman gardeners soon stumble across the truth of the garden theorem that the more lilies one plants in a group the greater the impact. In the garden a single lily may well be very attractive, but a group of three looks much more effective and natural. Single plants whet the appetite, bold groups provide a feast.

The argument is that it is better to plant a few bold groups of one type than get single bulbs of as many different kinds as possible, like the collector of matchbox lids or old masters. Gardeners have different temperaments. Some will be happy to plan their garden as a whole and to look at the broad canvas; the plants are loved and admired but they are seen as parts of the whole design. Others will use the garden first and foremost as a place to put interesting plants – they are plantsmen who enjoy examining the individual characteristics of their plants and their relationships with others of their genus and family. They may be just collectors of plants and finish with a cottage garden jumble. Madonna lilies in cottage gardens are a part of folk history. Lilies in this confetti mix will add more than a touch of exotic excitement.

Bold groups of lilies are more easily managed. Their sites are going to be more definite and less liable to the danger of intrusive fork or hoe. They can be fed and mulched more easily. Their floral contribution can be placed and timed to make the maximum contribution to the year-round garden plan. Early groups of *L. pyrenaicum* and *L. pumilum* are followed by the bold bedding Asiatics and the permanent *L. martagon* and kin. Trumpets and Americans see us through high summer and then in autumn *L. speciosum* and *L. auratum* with their hybrids come to

amaze. There are trumpet kinds that bloom late outside: the lovely *L. formosanum* and *L. philippinense*, although both thought of as cool greenhouse plants, are probably much hardier than normally thought and can bloom from mid summer until well into the autumn. I have had plants blooming very happily a month or two before Christmas. With *L. pyrenaicum* opening in late spring this means that six months at least are covered without any forcing or unnaturally delayed blooming.

POTTED LILIES

My wife has suggested that I have a dogmatic streak, but some things do need to be said clearly. There are two points to make about lilies in pots. First, almost every hybrid and very many of the species take to pots at least as easily as ducks take to water. There is no bulb easier to grow in containers. Second, by growing batches of lilies in pots, one can go in for instant gardening. Bulbs grown in pots can be brought to their flowering stations, on a patio or in a garden bed, just when they are getting to their most interesting stage. For those with large gardens, ferrying pots of lilies to flowering stations in the borders may seem a bother but as today's gardens are getting smaller and smaller, every square inch must be made to play its part and plants that have done their turn may have to make way for the next act. Lilies are ideal plants to wheel on to the stage in

Opposite: *Lilium hansonii is a robust lime-tolerant species with a range of fine offspring.*

late spring and through the summer. They are dramatic, colourful and real troupers.

There is a number of advantages to growing bulbs in pots and then positioning them when close to flowering. One is that under controlled conditions the bulbs can get into active life more quickly; slugs will not be able to ruin shoots; root systems can be fully expanded without being subject to frost and flood; uniform growth can be encouraged and feeding can be easily administered. These considerations are not to be too lightly dismissed as often bulbs arrive from dealers at awkward times, when there is thick snow on the ground or at least when it is pleasanter to work in the greenhouse or conservatory than out in the garden on sodden cold soil.

Another advantage of pot culture is that bulbs can be grown in batches. One can encourage them to grow quickly and provide bloom weeks or months earlier than normal. Alternatively it is possible to cold-store bulbs to delay them. Practically, it is possible to plant up the pots of growing bulbs in exactly the correct position, taking their heights and colours into consideration. Mistaken partnerships in the garden are more easily avoided, and unfortunate colour clashes should not happen.

LILIES FOR CUTTING

Lilies make marvellous cut flowers. They are superstars in the floral arrangement world, looking distinguished whether alone or in a mixed creation. A single stem in a straight-sided vase makes an exciting focal point. One, two or three stems in a vase can almost arrange themsleves. Asiatic hybrids with several blooms on a stem are already arranged. The complete beginner in 'floral art' will find lilies one of the easiest of flowers to manage.

Some will hesitate before cutting, knowing that bulbs need to recoup food from their leaves and stems. If only the flowering top is cut off there is no loss to the bulb, in fact this can concentrate activity in the foliage and benefit the bulb. The more leaves cut away the greater the deprivation of the bulb. Normally if half the stem is left there is not going to be much harm done.

Stems are best cut when the first flower is open, the rest will unfurl inside. Sometimes more opened heads will be cut but these need transporting inside carefully as conspicuous pollen can be dropped on the flowers, considerably spoiling their pristine appearance. Especially tragic are white flowers stained with pollen, like mascara smudging a fresh face.

When lifting lilies, small bulbs or bulblets can be removed and grown on in a spot where, if the flowers are taken, the garden display is not spoilt. Smaller bulbs can give pleasing flower heads, not so heavily crowded and so sometimes easier to display. If there is space in the vegetable patch this could be ideal. Alternatively groups of bulbs can be planted at the back of beds or borders to grow between shrubs where flower removal will not despoil the garden scene.

Whilst almost all lilies are excellent cut, some are especially effective. Of the species the little *L. pumilum* and *L. concolor* are dainty, the first in a nodding pose and the second with orange stars staring up at the sky. Of the species all the trumpets are lovely in a classic manner. *L. longiflorum* is the florist's favourite, the pure white one grown in large numbers from seed to provide pure white flowers especially favoured for Easter church decoration. Although commercially grown under glass this is not as tender as normally thought. In the garden the most popular and easy species is *L. regale*, white flowered with a golden throat but with buds heavily painted rich dark maroon. All these trumpets have rich perfumes.

The nodding blooms of most of the American species like *L. pardalinum* and the European *L. martagon* have a natural grace. These two species and some of their relatives are amongst the easiest of garden plants, lime tolerant ones that can be left down for ever and can be cut with reasonably long stems without taking away many leaves.

Hybrids are likely to be even easier plants to grow. Most popular with commercial growers and florists are the upright-facing Asiatic Hybrids like 'Enchantment'; they are so much easier to pack and they display their wares in the most obvious way. Of course they are lovely, but in the garden we can also choose hybrids that have flowers looking outwards or hanging, perhaps a more beguiling graceful pose. The golden Citronella Strain and the many subtly coloured North Hybrids can be breathtaking.

Stems carrying more than a single flower can last cut for a considerable time, a head will look well for over a week, a ten day spell of duty can easily be managed. Here the home grown article will often outpoint the bought stems that may have been cut rather early and have spent time in transit.

CHAPTER THREE

CHOOSING THE BEST: THE SPECIES

There are around 80 clearly defined species. Of these mention is made in this chapter of just over two dozen of the most reliable and rewarding kinds available, to be bought as bulbs or, in one or two cases which can be readily raised from easily obtained seeds.

Wild lilies are divided into seven groups of related plants. Each group has a number of features that show them to be more or less clearly divided from the rest of the genus.

Botanists look initially at seed germination methods, leaf arrangement, form of bulb scales, seed weight, bulb shape and habit, smooth or rough petals, flower form and the bulb colour. Each group will be discussed and then its members described in alphabetical order. They are as follows:

1. Martagon Group	**5. Asian Group**
L. hansonii	*L. cernuum*
L. martagon	*L. concolor*
	L. davidii
2. American Group	*L. henryi*
L. canadense	*L. lancifolium –*
L. michiganense	*(L. tigrinum)*
L. pardalinum	*L. nepalense*
L. p. giganteum	*L. pumilum –*
L. superbum	*(L. tenuifolium)*
3. Candidum Group	**6. Trumpet Group**
L. candidum	*L. formosanum*
L. monadelphum –	*L. longiflorum*
(L. szovitsianum)	*L. regale*
L. pyrenaicum	**7. Dauricum**
4. Oriental Group	**Group**
L. auratum	*L. dauricum*
L. speciosum	

MARTAGON GROUP

This group of lilies is one that all gardeners can enjoy regardless of their soil. They are completely lime tolerant and are some of the hardiest of all the family. There have been a number of places where *L. martagon* has felt so at home in Britain and elsewhere that it has naturalized itself from seed. They are long-lived plants that will put up with much poorer soils and conditions than many others.

They are characterized by having their shiny foliage arranged in whorls at distinct intervals up the stem. There may be up to 15 leaves arranged like the spokes of a wheel in each whorl. The flowers are of quite modest size but they are plentiful.

L. hansonii
This is a very hardy strong plant growing to around 1.2 m (4 ft) tall. It may come taller in partial shade and this may well be the place for it as the flowers retain their best colour and the plants seem to grow better. Happily it is very virus resistant.

Flowering in early and mid summer, its blooms are displayed as a loose pyramid of a dozen or more medium sized nodding pale orange flowers, the petals recurving to point upwards. The tangerine is enlivened with dark spots, but almost the most noticeable feature of the flowers is their very thick waxy or plastic-like texture.

Polished dark green leaves are handsomely displayed in whorls at relatively short intervals up the strong stems. Individual leaves are of clean pointed elliptical form. It is very long lived: plants may well last for 50 years. It is a stem-rooting type and benefits from deep planting; up to 20 cm (8 in) could well be in order. Bulbs once settled will split steadily into decent sized ones; other smaller bulblets may well form on the underground stem and it will easily increase from scales. Seeds are formed readily from crossing with *L. martagon*, though less freely from its own pollen. Lime tolerant.

L. martagon Martagon lily

This is the hardiest of lilies in Britain. In the wild it is the most widespread. It grows well on a wide variety of soils and is perfectly at home on lime.

It stands 1–2 m (3–6 ft) tall, depending on the strength of the bulb and the clone. Bulbs split slowly over the years, but it spreads itself by seeding. Copious amounts of seed are set and float around the site. Seedlings take some years to reach flowering size but when happy and not harassed by constant hoeing will develop to form colonies.

New shoots grow rapidly through spring to be in bloom for weeks from early summer. A new bulb's first flowering effort may be restricted to half a dozen smallish curled up mauve–pink blooms, but an established plant can produce a stem with 50 flowers. Each thick petal curls up into a cylinder and, though each individual bloom is small, the effect of a group with lots on each stem can be very effective, a haze of pinky mauve. There are ivory white forms and very dark aubergine ones. They come with greater or lesser amounts of spotting.

Up to 15 or 16 leaves are arranged in whorls at distinct intervals up the stem, in most forms being more widely separated than in *L. hansonii*. A few scattered leaves may be added.

This is a plant to place in its permanent home and leave alone. It does well between shrubs or in light woodland, where it should be given a chance to seed itself. It can also be grown in meadow-like conditions or in the wild garden. Indifferent to lime.

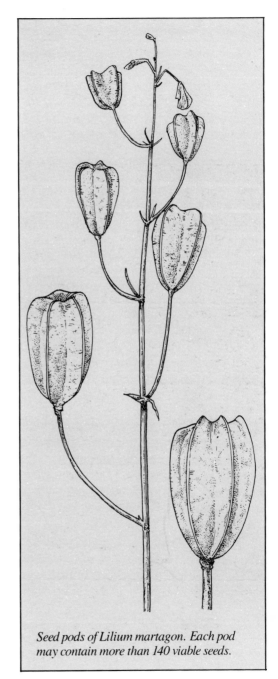

Seed pods of Lilium martagon. Each pod may contain more than 140 viable seeds.

AMERICAN GROUP

Many of the species of this group are closely related and do not look all that different from the martagons when out of bloom. Most have the same whorled foliage and strong stems. They usually have pendant flowers, often with strongly recurved petals.

L. canadense

This is not the strongest of the group, though it has been grown in Europe for about 360 years. It is worth trying as it is one of the most elegant of all. Firm upright stems reach 1–2 m (3–6 ft) with whorls of bright green pointed foliage and wide pyramids of flowers in mid summer.

Pedicels holding the individual blooms slope out from the stem at about 30 degrees and then bend to let the flowers hang downwards, a beautiful sculptured shape. Petals start close together, forming a narrow trumpet, but then sweep evenly out to point horizontally. Petals will be 5–6 cm (2–2½ in) long. The usual form is a clear lemon-gold but there are orange ones. As the blooms are widely spaced and there may be from six to over 20 on a stem the effect of a single stem is delightful. Groups are bewitching.

It is a species that hates lime and finds winter wet so depressing that it may die. Excellent drainage is a prerequisite for success, but in the spring when growing strongly it needs plentiful water. Where it feels at home it will increase by sending out stolons perhaps 13 cm (5 in) below ground, forming a fresh bulb at the end of each. Lime hater.

L. michiganense

This is closely related to *L. canadense* with much of its graceful habit, whorled neat foliage, upward reaching flower pedicels, and hanging flowers. Mature plants stand some 1.2–1.5 m (4–5 ft) high with three to 20 blooms to a stem.

There is some variation in flower colour but the usual is a good orange with the lower third of each petal heavily spotted. The petals of the hanging blooms recurve more strongly than those of *L. canadense*.

Seeds grow well and as the flowers are a reasonable size are worth trying. Also a lime hater.

L. pardalinum   Leopard lily

This lily and the next are easily the toughest of all American lilies, growing well in most gardens in any soil. Stems grow from 1.2–2.4 m (4–8 ft) tall and have strong dark polished leaves in whorls. The bulbs are rhizomatous; they form scaly mats some 15 cm (6 in) below the surface and will bud off fresh growths each year so that, where there was one flowering stem the first year, the next season there may be two, three, four, or even five.

The plant will make a fine stand in a few years, stems being roughly 10–20 cm (4–8 in) apart.

Flowers are painted a rich gold bordering orange and have petal tips generously painted crimson. Dark maroon spotting justifies its common name, and these spots are particularly dense towards the base. Petals recurve almost into circles, the flowers looking like exotic lanterns.

In nature it is a variable species, but

Magnificent Lilium auratum displays large flowers 20–25 cm (8–10 in) across.

in cultivation the bulbs increase so quickly that relatively few clones probably figure in the whole representation of the species. It will grow better in moister spots than many other American lilies although of course it does not relish stagnant water. Lime tolerant.

L. pardalinum giganteum   Sunset lily

This is a natural hybrid of L. par- dalinum, a very strong grower with robust rhizomatous bulbs that increase quickly so that a single piece soon forms a stand with a forest of canes standing 2–2.4 m (6–8 ft) high with stylized whorled foliage and lots of hanging blooms.

Flowers have long-pointed petals severely recurved and painted in bright colours. The basic tangerine gold is enlivened with dark maroon spots, some of which may be circled, while the petal tips are a deep crimson scarlet.

Bulbs grow in almost any soil in- cluding heavy clay. Lime tolerant.

L. superbum

Habit of growth of this fine lily is similar to that of L. canadense but may look a little stouter. Stems may reach 1.2–2.4 m (4–8 ft) and carry a few or up to three dozen blooms. These vary in colour but are usually orange tipped with crimson. Vivid red anthers add to the display as does the central little green star formed by the nectary furrows. Centres are not difficult to see as the petals curl back. Blooms are well spaced, the whole spike being at its best rather later than its relatives, in mid to late summer.

Bulbs need acid soil. In growth they like plenty of water. Happy bulbs divide freely to send out stolons with new bulbs forming at their ends. Lime hater.

CANDIDUM GROUP

Members of this group are found from the Himalayas across into Europe, where there are more of this group than of any other, although they have be- come very scarce due to collecting, the increase of agriculture and the depreda- tions of goats and sheep. All have scattered leaves, orthodox rounded bulbs, and are only rarely found with any stem rooting.

L. candidum   Madonna lily

Only the tiger lily could possibly challenge this lily as having the longest association with human culture. Early on it became associated with Christian symbolism but before this it had been used as a decorative motif on vases and frescoes predating Christianity by at least 1500 years.

Good forms stand 90 cm–1.5 m (3–5 ft) high with outward-facing wide pure white bells with the golden pollen emphasizing their purity. Strong stems can carry a dozen flowers in mid summer.

It is unusual in several respects. It maintains a rosette of leaves through the autumn and winter. In spring the flowering stem arises and is crowded with leaves at the bottom but these become smaller and fewer as the flowers are reached.

Unlike any other lily its largish bulbs prefer to be planted shallowly, their tips only just being covered. It prefers well drained soil with lime in it. It is best kept separate from any other lily as it catches viruses with great ease and may be troubled with botrytis in bad seasons or in wet, rather airless spots. Once happy it should be left alone. Likes lime.

p 29

L. monadelphum   (L. szovitsianum)

It is the present fashion to place the plant *L. szovitsianum* into this species. Botanically this may be correct but from the garden point of view they have distinguishing features. They come from the Caucasus hills and are handsome garden plants growing to 1.2–1.5 m (4–5 ft) with large wide recurving bells of yellow, *L. monadelphum* being a deeper shade than the usual *L. szovitsianum*. Each bloom is about 10 cm (4 in) across and more or less pendant. Stems usually carry three to six flowers, though capable of more. Both are open through early and mid summer. *L. szovitsianum* seems to be a shade easier and more prolific in bloom. It can be quickly distinguished by its rust-coloured pollen in contrast to the yellow of *L. monadelphum*.

   L. szovitsianum is possibly the easier of the two complexes of plants, though neither is difficult once it has settled in. They may be sulky for their first year. These are plants to place in a permanent spot. Place them in semi-shade in a spot where you will be able to enjoy them for the next 10 to 40 years. They do not object to lime and grow well on heavy soils. Once established they may take to seeding themselves,

a real compliment to a gardener. Lime tolerant.

L. pyrenaicum

This easy little lily grows rapidly in the spring and can be in bloom in late spring. Its hardiness is such that it has on occasion jumped the garden fence.

   Stems reach from 30 cm–1.2 m (1–4 ft) but are normally between these extremes. They are well clothed with upward reaching narrow leaves. Hanging flowers with petals curled back into balls are a bright yellow, perhaps slightly greenish and much spotted with black dots.

   Most of us are inclined to have a sniff at lilies to find out if they are perfumed. You will probably realize this is ill-advised well before you get too near to this one – its odour is less than pleasing.

   Bulbs are large and can be planted permanently and deeply, with 15 cm (6 in) of soil over their tops and then left alone. They are not fussy, will grow with lime, and appreciate reasonable drainage.

ORIENTAL GROUP

Only two species are dealt with here, but many would put them jointly at the top of the beauty parade. They are two of the latest to bloom, lime haters, and strong stem-rooting kinds.

L. auratum   Japanese golden rayed lily

In a genus where splendour is commonplace, this stands out as quite magnificent. Forms vary in height from 75 cm–2.4 m (30 in–8 ft). Virus-free bulbs grow strongly with very robust stems

Above: Lilium concolor is an easy, small Asian species with an upward-gazing pose.

Opposite: Lilium speciosum 'Rubrum' is a richly coloured form of a Japanese species.

holding from three or four to over 30 blooms.

Wide star-shaped flowers look outwards and measure up to 25–30 cm (10–12 in) across. They look miraculous and have one of the most powerful and pleasing perfumes in the plant kingdom. What are taken to be the type flowers are waxy white ones with a central stripe of gold, 'auratum' meaning decorated with gold. They are further ornamented with crimson spots. There are forms with the central stripe starting gold but quickly becoming crimson and somewhat suffusing the white of the petals. The spots of some are dramatically larger.

Leaves are many, tough, long-pointed and narrow, crowded along the stem, being smaller as they approach the flower head.

Bulbs are usually grown in pots because they seem so exotic. They will be killed by lime, and are relatively late blooming. They are hardy outside where they will bloom in late summer and early autumn. Sometimes outside they are so late they really have little time to die back before the winter. They require very well drained soil. Gritty open soil mixes suit them best. In nature they grow in soil derived from volcanic ash and very little else. Do not overfeed them.

While hardy, they dislike excessive wet through the winter and bulbs fall prey to virus very easily. If you start with healthy rooted bulbs you stand a good chance of success at least for a season or so, but remember, no lime. Planted with 20 cm (8 in) of friable gritty soil over their tops the stems will root vigorously and massively augment the work of the basal roots.

L. speciosum

Blooming in early and mid autumn outside, this species is probably best in pots in northern Europe and similar climates. It blooms at anything from 60 cm–1.5 m (2–5 ft) tall. In milder warmer spots it may be tried in acid conditions in semi-shade where in leafy soils it can make a most distinctive stand with its plain attractive foliage stylishly held on stalks cutting clean shapes in the air before the first buds appear. It grows to 75 cm–1.5 m (30 in–5 ft).

Flowers are widely spaced and posed at half pendant angles to suggest oriental grace. Petals recurve to point back and upwards and are white but flushed pink and dotted crimson, especially on the papillae (raised fleshy points). The amount of crimson-red colouring varies. Some forms have the basic white flushed crimson pink, others are almost completely crimson.

Planted in lime-free compost or soil the plants grow easily. It makes a fine pot plant. A single stem will perfume a room.

ASIAN GROUP

This is a large group with more divergent characteristics than most other groups. Most of those listed here have certain characteristics in common. They have scattered leaves, rounded bulbs and turkscap flowers.

L. cernuum

This is a small lily growing only 45–

75 cm (18–30 in) high. It blooms in mid summer, sometimes a little earlier. It has very rolled back petals in pendant flowers rather like those of *L. pumilum* (see p. 51) but coloured a mauvey pink rather similar to the shades of some paler martagons now busy making seed pods. They are scented.

The small bulbs grow happily in well drained soil, being relatively deeply planted as this is a strong stem rooter. It grows quickly from seed, which it would be wise to sow in batches, as this is not necessarily a long-lived bulb. It does not object to lime.

L. concolor

This is another small charmer, from only 30–75 cm (12–30 in) high. Thin wiry stems with dark narrow leaves hold a number of wide almost flat stars of bright orange, facing upwards, an unusual pose for this group. You can get them plain or spotted. Three or four up to a splendid ten flowers can be produced per stem. It makes a lovely garden plant, a charming pot lily and a very attractive cut flower. Lime tolerant.

L. davidii

With strong upright dark stems reaching 90 cm–1.2 m (3–4 ft) high when blooming in mid summer this fine plant is well furnished with very many narrow-pointed dark leaves. They become smaller higher up the stem. Where the leaves join the stem there is often some silky hairiness. This same silky sheen covers the flower buds – as many as twenty or more hung out at the end of horizontal flower stalks. Flowers are rather like those of the tiger lily, *L. lancifolium*, but are rather smaller and more polished. *L. davidii*'s bright colouring of orange scarlet is decorated by raised black spots. Petals 8 cm (3 in) long recurve like those of the martagon lily.

There is quite a bit of variation in the species, the most distinct probably being *L. d. willmottiae*. This has similar dark stems and many narrow leaves. It is usually much more prolific in bloom and while the stems are quite wiry they arch over. It can easily have 30 to 40 shining bright orange flowers with dark spots. This load does mean that it welcomes support, either some natural support from shrubs like rosemary or a stake. The flowers are certainly worth the trouble. One can place firm stakes at planting time, hoping to get them in the right spot, or take the lesser risk by waiting until the stems have grown, then plunging them into the ground hoping to avoid the bulbs and the stems below ground. It is best to place the stake on the side to which the stem is leaning as growth from the bulb is slightly eccentric. In spring the stem emerges from the bulb and spears its way sideways before slanting towards the surface and the open air. This is something that the type may also do but probably never so energetically as *L. d. willmottiae*.

It is best planted deeply in soil enriched with humus and enlivened with grit. The stem below ground may foster several useful young bulbs along its length. Just about lime tolerant but enjoys an abundance of humus.

Opposite: *The showiest forms of the well-known tiger lily,* Lilium lancifolium *(formerly L. tigrinum) grow strongly on all soils.*
Left: Lilium formosanum, *an elegant species belonging to the Far East Trumpet group, is probably hardier than its reputation would suggest.*
Below: Lilium nepalense *is an exotic and dramatic lily, yet it is relatively easy to grow from seed.*

L. henryi

This is one of the hardiest of all lilies, persisting after years of neglect which would make others sulk and depart. Fat bulbs produce strong stems reaching up and then arching, from 1.2–2.1 m (4–7 ft) high. Thick polished leaves are dark green, a picture of health. Six to 12 blooms in late summer are average, but exceptional stems may have up to 30. Colour is a tangerine-orange with some darker spots and with green nectary furrows towards the centre. The flowers hang with petals curved back so that the raised points of the lower parts are made noticeable.

Colour fades in the sun, so it makes sense to grow it in partial shade, perhaps between shrubs or trees. It is a strong yeoman bulb with a vigorous propensity to stem rooting and it seems to enjoy some lime in the soil.

L. lancifolium   Tiger lily

It seems strange to have to address this old favourite by this name. *L. tigrinum* comes more naturally after all these years but nothing is for ever in this world, especially the botanical world.

It stands 1.5–1.8 m (5–6 ft) tall, a strong growing lily with dark wiry stems, lots of scattered narrow dark leaves, many bulbils forming in the leaf axils, and many bright orange hanging flowers with much spotting. It is one of the main species used in the breeding of the Asiatic Hybrids. It is susceptible to virus and too often the stocks distributed are infected, but it is such a strong plant that it can often survive for several seasons while hosting the disease. This is, of course, calamitous: it grows and flowers while at the same time providing a renewable reservoir of virus with which to infect all the lilies within aphid flight.

Stands of clean stock can look most impressive in late summer and early autumn when each stem may have a dozen nodding brightly coloured flowers with petals recurving backwards almost in a complete circle and clearly displaying the purple-black freckling. Outstanding stems may have two or even three dozen flowers. Selections have been made from the species, the most commonly offered being the somewhat larger, more robust *L. l. splendens*. There is a yellow form too, *L. l. flaviflorum*. Most of the cultivated kinds are triploids and these can be grown in any soils, but the type and *L. l. flaviflorum* are diploids and are very much more at home in acid conditions.

L. nepalense

This is one of the most wonderful of the group. It has been grown successfully in Britain and, while nobody would suggest that it is one of the easiest, it can be grown satisfactorily. Common sense can help a lot and it is certainly such a fine thing that it ought to be tried. Bulbs and seeds are normally available.

Plants get into growth later than almost any lily, the shoots emerging from the bulbs and wandering below ground before making for the surface and producing up to 90 cm (3 ft) stems. They do not have very many leaves, these having marked parallel veining, rather like those of some of the smaller hostas. New bulblets form on the horizontal stems below ground.

Two or three large flowers hang downwards. The colour is an unusual greeny yellow but stained inside a rich mahogany-purple from the centre for three-quarters of their length. The shape underlines their distinctiveness. From the stem the petals form a narrow funnel and then open out to point horizontally. As petals may be 15 cm (6 in) long, the whole is most impressive.

It blooms in late summer and to finish growing it needs some weeks of reasonable warm weather after the flowers fade. While in growth it can take quite a bit of moisture, but in winter it is better on the dry side. With its wandering habit and late flowering it could be something to try in a bed in the cool greenhouse. It needs to be grown in a very open humus-rich soil without any lime.

L. pumilum (L. tenuifolium) Coral lily

This may be better known to many as *L. tenuifolium*, under which name it still appears in catalogues, although this name was superseded over four decades ago.

L. pumilum is a small easy lily flowering from very small bulbs not much bigger than marbles. It grows 30–60 cm (1–2 ft) high with from one to 20 curled up nodding flowers in brilliant coral scarlet. The arrangement is in a narrow spike. This display occurs in early summer, but in pots it is easy to bring forward to spring. Leaves are

many and tend to clasp the stem and become smaller as they reach the flowers.

If flowers are prevented from seeding, the bulbs usually have a longer life than if allowed to give a very bountiful harvest. Seeds germinate well and can be grown to flowering in two or three seasons with no trouble. Lime tolerant.

TRUMPET GROUP

These are everyone's idea of the classic lily. The best known, *L. regale*, was only introduced into Britain in 1905 and was named in 1912. The different species vary considerably in their longevity. They are characterized by their scattered leaves, largish round bulbs and trumpet-shaped flowers. They are stem rooters.

L. formosanum

Blooming late in the summer it can have trouble in getting through its full growing programme before winter arrives again, but it is probably a lot hardier than generally thought. For several seasons I have had this and *L. longiflorum* growing outside where they have withstood both wet and cold much better than might have been expected.

Depending on the form, the slender but wiry stems may reach anything from a diminutive 15 cm (6 in) or so, to an impressive 2 m (6 ft). The trumpet flowers start with a very narrow funnel which is maintained for a good distance before it gently expands to the widely flared mouth. Inside all is sparkling white purity, outside the petals are more

Above: *The florist's lily, L. longiflorum, growing happily in the author's garden.*

Opposite: *The regal lily, L. regale, admired for its ease and beauty since its arrival in 1905.*

or less overpainted in dark wine colours. One can just see the suspicion of this from the inside. Flowers are impressively long and are held horizontally.

L. f. pricei is the dwarf form, which blooms possibly three weeks to a month earlier. It is usually thought to be hardier; it certainly has longer to get its growing done and the bulbs matured. It reaches from around a meagre 15 cm (6 in) to the dizzy height of 60 cm (2 ft).

This species sets abundant seeds, though you may have to cut the pods and finish ripening inside. Seeds germinate quickly and flowering plants are a possibility the same year! Lime tolerant.

L. longiflorum   Easter lily

This is the white lily of the florists, often used for church decoration for the Easter festival. It has large white flowers with possibly a touch of green but no bibulous wine colouring. Outside it grows from 45–90 cm (18 in–3 ft) tall, under glass it may be taller.

It is normally thought of as a greenhouse lily where a single flower will scent the house, but I have successfully grown some hundreds outside for several years in an open field of sandy soil. Outside it blooms in late summer. Inside it can be brought into bloom almost any time, depending on how the bulbs are treated. From readily available seeds, bulbs can reach flowering in a matter of months. Lime tolerant.

L. regale   Regal lily

Of the trumpet species this is the easiest, hardiest and, most unbiased observers would say, the best. If you are only growing one trumpet species in the garden this should be your choice. Depending on age and circumstances it will flower at 60 cm–1.8 m (2–6 ft) high.

Opening in mid summer, the dark stems, well clad with dark shining leaves, may hold 10, 20 or up to 30 large blooms. The sight and perfume are quite magnificent. The type has large long buds of a mahogany-wine colour which open to reveal silken dazzling white interiors with golden honeyed throats. The perfume is present in an invisible cloud around the plants. Displays will last well into late summer.

Seeds germinate freely and if looked after the young bulbs grow rapidly. It is possible to have them produce maiden blooms within eighteen months. It could be good policy to nip off these first blooms and concentrate on fattening the bulbs to produce greater bounty the following season. Lime tolerant.

DAURICUM GROUP

L. dauricum

This is a very hardy lily from northern Russia, north-eastern China and Korea, as well as some Japanese islands.

Fat strong stems reach upwards 60–90 cm (2–3 ft) and display perhaps half a dozen large wide upward-facing bowl-shaped flowers. While very narrow at the base so that there is air between them, the petals then expand to have wide blades. Usual colouring is golden at the centre becoming orange and red, darker towards the tips. Good forms are most impressive. This is one of the founders of the upward-facing race of hybrids, but is worth growing for its own sake. It blooms in early and mid summer. Lime tolerant.

In Europe the species *L. bulbiferum* and its popular form *L.b. croceum* are of very similar character to *L. dauricum*. They are presently classified with the Candidum group but their appearance makes it clear that there is a close relationship, the two species must have been differentiated from a common ancestor and then gone their own ways geographically. They hybridize easily. Flowers of *L. bulbi-ferum* are cup or bowl shaped and look upwards, the type being a rich orange red, *L.b. croceum* being more orange.

Early hybrids were grown under Latin names. Various series of hybrids were grown as *L. × maculatum*, probably originating from the early interbreeding in Japan of *L. dauricum* and *L. concolor*. Races of hybrids of the same origin were introduced as *L. × elegans* and *L. × thunbergianum*. These were crossed with *L. bulbiferum* to produce races under the names *L. × hollandicum* and *L. × umbellatum*.

It is the two species, *L. dauricum* and *L. bulbiferum*, that together with *L. lancifolium* (*L. tigrinum*) are the founder species for Jan de Graaff's Mid-Century hybrids such as 'Enchantment' and 'Destiny' – the mainspring for most further breeding of Asiatic Hybrids.

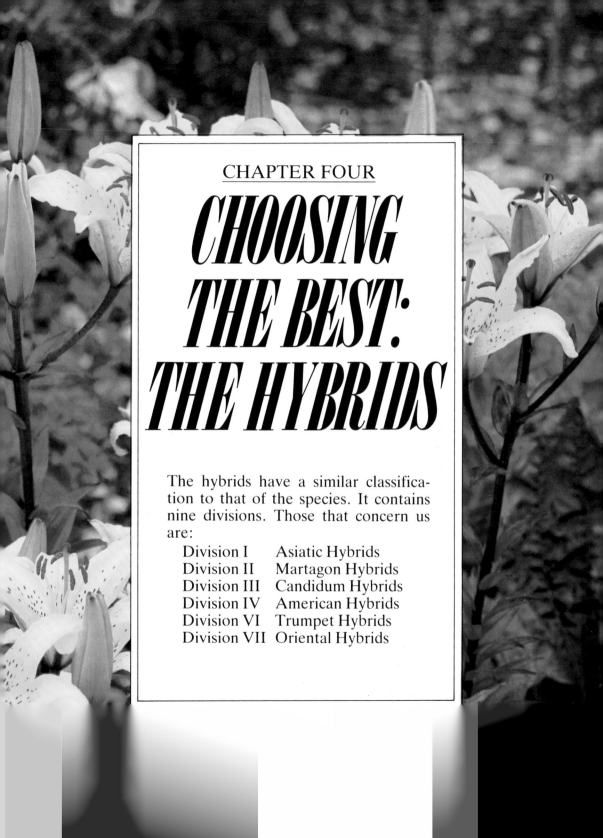

CHAPTER FOUR

CHOOSING THE BEST: THE HYBRIDS

The hybrids have a similar classification to that of the species. It contains nine divisions. Those that concern us are:

Division I   Asiatic Hybrids
Division II   Martagon Hybrids
Division III   Candidum Hybrids
Division IV   American Hybrids
Division VI   Trumpet Hybrids
Division VII Oriental Hybrids

DIVISION I. ASIATIC HYBRIDS

This is by far the largest division, including all the popular kinds used for the garden and cut flowers, such as 'Enchantment'. They have been derived from interbreeding many kinds, including *L. bulbiferum, dauricum, lancifolium, davidii, pumilum, concolor,* and early hybrid races derived mainly from these species. To bring a little more order into this crowded division, it has been divided into three sections: (A) with flowers that are upward facing; (B) with outward-facing blooms and (C) with pendant or downward-facing blooms.

Most are more or less lime-tolerant. *L. lankongense* hybrids should be given lime-free conditions.

□ASIATIC HYBRIDS: UPWARD-FACING

'APELDOORN'
Strong upright hybrid reaching some 90 cm (3 ft) in mid summer with plenty of bright green leaves and wide heads of bright orange stars. Flowers thick textured and spotted purple black. Bred from *L. davidii* crossed with a selected clone 'Erect', from the old upward-facing Dutch Hybrid race, *L. × hollandicum*. Flower spacing makes this one of the better orange types.

'CHINOOK'
Bred in Oregon from a longish line of breeding but with 'Enchantment' as father, from which it is very distinct. It has a well-spaced pyramid of blooms standing 90 cm–1.2 m (3–4 ft) high. Warm shades of orange, buff and apricot mingle pleasantly to make this one of the most pleasing of mid summer flowerers.

'CINNABAR'
This was among the first of the Mid-Century Hybrids to be introduced as the result of Jan de Graaff's breeding work in Oregon. It is a sturdy plant 75–90 cm (30 in–3 ft) high with rather crowded heads of dark maroon.

'CONNECTICUT KING'
Millions of these invade our florists' shops each year. It is a bold strong plant with plenty of shiny bright green leaves pointing somewhat upwards and large opened stars of bright gold. It was one of the results of much work undertaken to breed strong upward-facing yellow lilies without spots. I prefer the yellows with spots but certainly 'Connecticut King' is a very successful robust flower. The rich yellow is darker towards the centre. It stands 75–90 cm (30 in–3 ft) and blooms in early and mid summer.

'CORINA'
'Cinnabar' is the mother of this flower but the colour is much softer, the broad stars being crimson-pink flushed red and dotted chestnut-mahogany in the centre. It is usually in bloom by early summer, standing 75–90 cm (30 in–3 ft) with firm stems and darker leaves than some.

'DESTINY'
Introduced in 1950 as one of the Mid-Century Hybrids, this is still much admired. Its wide bowls of lemon-gold

flowers are attractively dotted dark chocolate. It blooms in early summer at about 75 cm (30 in) high.

'ENCHANTMENT'
There have been more bulbs grown of this than any other lily in cultivation. Millions are sold as cut flowers each year and similar huge quantities are planted in gardens. It is likely to be the first lily a newcomer grows. It has shiny bright green leaves and a close head of wide pointing starry flowers of a very bright orange with a sprinkling of small dark spots. Early summer, 75–90 cm (30 in–3 ft) high.

'ESTHER'
Looks and is a strong healthy lily. Strong dark stems with shiny leaves, both perhaps with a certain amount of silken hairiness. Flowers are well distributed in a conical head and are a rich orange-red shade, slightly paler in the base where there are a number of purple-brown spots. Firm texture and glossy finish make the whole sparkle with freshness. Early through mid summer, 75–90 cm (30 in–3 ft) high.

'FESTIVAL'
This distinctive lily blooms in mid rather than early summer and has very dark stems and leaves. Leaf axils are crowded with huge quantities of bulbils, in the tiger lily manner. Dark long-pointed mahogany buds open to make clean pointed stars. While the petal centres are a bright yellow quite lavishly decorated with dark spots, the tips and the edges are a rich bronze. It is dramatic and different. 90 cm–1.2 m (3–4 ft) high.

'FIRECRACKER'
This has a pyramid of very many relatively small flowers of unfading rich cherry red, its numbers making most impressive 90 cm–1.2 m (3–4 ft) stems in early and mid summer.

'HARMONY'
Dating back to the first of the Mid-Century Hybrids but still a useful and attractive kind, noticeably less tall than some later bred kinds. It only needs about 60 cm (2 ft) to display its wares, a few large wide bowls of a very pleasing amber shade. Having made this wide bowl, the petals recurve a little. Spotting is reserved, just a few small dark ones. It blooms in early summer.

'HERITAGE'
Clean-looking with pale stems and light green leaves below a pyramid of up to 20 blooms of glowing orange-red, slightly paler in the centre at the nectary furrows. As the flowers are large it can be a most impressive lily; petals may measure 10 cm (4 in) long by at least 4 cm (1½ in) wide. It flowers from early to mid summer. 75–90 cm (30 in–3 ft) high.

'MEDAILLON' ('MEDALLION')
So far all those described have been yellow or orange; this is a cooler coloured kind. Stiff stems carry large wide-spaced bowl-shaped blooms of a pale creamy yellow but with a central reservoir of darker pigmentation, an old gold verging on pale orange, but this is not a glaring shade. It flowers in early and mid summer, 75–90 cm (30 in–3 ft) high.

Opposite: *'Connecticut King' is a very robust and showy florist's lily that performs equally well as a border plant.*

Above: *'Corina' is more subtly coloured than many Asiatics. It is dark leaved and glows with health.*

'MONT BLANC'

Large-flowered and sturdy with wide-petalled stars of white with relatively few small dark spots. Good clean shiny foliage helps make a plant of pleasing contrast to the hot colours. Early and mid summer, 75–90 cm (30 in–3 ft) high.

'PIRATE'

Dark wiry stems and similarly dark narrow pointed leaves with medium-sized flowers in well-spaced heads. Dark burgundy or mahogany buds open to form pointed stars of brilliant red and orange, made all the more effective by the dark freckling and the very high gloss lacquer finish. Most effective garden plant and very good cut bloom. Early summer, 75–90 cm (30 in–3 ft) high.

'PROMINENCE'

Strong easy cultivar with wide umbel of pinky orange stars. Dark healthy, narrow foliage. Height 75 cm (30 in).

'RED NIGHT'

This is also known as 'Roter Cardinal', one of the darkest of all the section. Leaves and stems are dark, the green being overlaid with purple. Flowers are of a good size and a starry bowl shape; the colour is a brooding deep wine-red with an admixture of purple brown. Some may find it a little too dark but it makes a handsome contrast to lighter neighbours. Mid summer, 90 cm (3 ft) high.

'ROSITA'

This has *L. cernuum* as its father and its influence can be seen in the long narrow foliage and the colour of the flowers.

These are pleasant shades of mauve-pink. As they develop the colour changes from pale buffs to darker mauves. It is far removed from the sturdy crowded stance of 'Enchantment'; stems, leaves and flowers are altogether more graceful, a legacy of *L. cernuum*. Flowers are star-shaped and have plenty of air around them. Mid summer, 75–90 cm (30 in–3 ft) high.

'STERLING STAR'

This has some of the quality of the last listed; its foliage is long and narrow, stems are dark and the star-shaped flowers are widely and pleasingly spaced. Blooms appear to float in the air, looking up in frank wide-eyed innocence made all the more telling by its sprinkling of dark dots. Early and mid summer, 75–90 cm (30 in–3 ft) high.

'SUNRAY'

This comes from the same parentage as 'Connecticut King' but has its lemon-gold enlivened with a soupçon of brown freckles. Its stems are stout, the leaves polished rich green and the flowers thick-textured and boldly posed. In the garden I prefer it to 'Connecticut King'. It flowers from early and mid summer, 75 cm (30 in) high.

'TAMARA'

A pleasing kind with lots of medium-sized blooms in well spaced heads. Colours are a mixture; the centre is of pastel amber shades flecked with mauve-pink but gives way to warmer red-inspired shades at the extremities. Mid summer, 75–90 cm (30 in–3 ft) high.

'WHITE PRINCE'
Perhaps the finest white Asiatic.
Noticeably broad petals forming large
stars of pure white when fully open but
somewhat creamy in bud. The flowers
are unspotted but have the pale brown
anthers to give a contrast and the
nectary furrows in the centre are
creamy. One of the earlier kinds. Sturdy
stems. 90 cm (3 ft) high.

□ASIATIC HYBRIDS: OUTWARD-FACING

'ATTILA'
Strong-growing dark-stemmed kind
with glowing orange-red flowers with
recurving petals. Decorated with
chocolate-purple spots. Early and mid
summer, 75–90 cm (30 in–3 ft) high.

'BINGO'
One of the dwarfest of the Asiatics and
so sometimes used for pot work. It
grows only 30–45 cm (12–18 in) high with
coloured stems and 10 cm (4 in) wide
flowers of orange-red with paler throats.
With perhaps three to six blooms on a
stem, it can look very impressive in
early and mid summer.

'BRANDYWINE'
Introduced in 1953 and still going
strong. A broad-petalled wide almost
flat flower with petal tips gently
recurving. Tawny orange with darker
red spots making crowded colourful
spikes 90 cm (3 ft) tall.

'CORSAGE'
One of the unusual hybrids with no
pollen and so useful for corsages.
Flowers are of only medium size but

there are plenty of them on stems that
will reach 90 cm–1.2 m (3–4 ft) high.
Colours are a medley; in bud they are
creamy buffs, they then open to pale
pink with a white middle but yellowish
ivory suffused with pink on the outside.
Long lasting in bloom, starting in early
summer.

'EXCEPTION'
This is another without pollen, but
much darker than 'Corsage'. It has a lot
of *L. cernuum* blood in it. Flowers
appear to be made of marble, thick-
textured and firm. Colours are dark
maroon-red but with a white centre. It is
an unusual colouring and an unusual
looking lily. It can look artificial, but
there may be places where it could be a
conversation piece, and having no
pollen makes it useful for flower
arranging and for pot work. Early and
mid summer, 90 cm (3 ft) high.

'FIRE KING'
This is a very old hybrid but still retains
its vigour. It crowds its stems with
wide-petalled blooms of vivid deep
orange with dark spots. Stout strong
stems. Early and mid summer, 90 cm
(3 ft) high.

'KING PETE'
Bold, large, yellow flower, shading to
tangerine in the centre. Large spikes on
sturdy stems. Polished, bright green
foliage. Height 75 cm (30 in).

'MOULIN ROUGE'
Taller than most, with spaced flowers of
rich orange but splashed with darker
shades giving an overall darker effect.
Mid summer, 90 cm–1.2 m (3–4 ft) high.

The famous 'Enchantment' has been grown in millions as a cut flower and garden plant.

'Harmony' is unusually early and dwarf in bloom and has played a large part in breeding.

'PAPRIKA'

This has held a place for 30 years. Broad-petalled, firm-textured flowers are a burnt dark red shade with a more matt finish than some. Sturdy and only 50–75 cm (20–30 in) high. Mid summer.

□ ASIATIC HYBRIDS: DOWNWARD-FACING

These, with their pendant pose and taller stems, are altogether more graceful than the other Asiatics. Unless otherwise stated they start flowering in mid summer. They will enjoy deep cool root runs. The *L. lankongense* hybrids are usually nicely scented, a quality that most Asiatics lack.

'ANGELA NORTH'

Standing 1.2–1.5 m (4–5 ft), stems are slender but strong with narrow foliage and lots of widely spaced pendant blooms arranged in a pyramid. Petals recurve, displaying their rich mauvey pink colour. Hybrid of *L. lankongense*. Avoid lime.

'ARIADNE'

A wonderful lily which can have from one to three dozen small flowers of curled turkscap shape hanging in a pyramid that may reach 2 m (6 ft) high. The blossom is a mixture of pastel shades, buds being a pale apricot or salmon but opening to a mixture of pale tangerine with white and pink, this mauve pink being darker at the petal tips. Peppered with orange-brown spots. Scented. Bred from *L. lankongense*, crossed with the old hybrid 'Maxwill'. Avoid lime with this beautiful lily.

'BARBARA NORTH' P 80

This is a very pleasant pink-flowered *L. lankongense* hybrid about 1.2–1.5 m (4–5 ft) high with well spaced blooms. Avoid lime.

CITRONELLA P 81

This is a strain not a clone, so that there is some variation, noticeably in the size of the flowers and the amount of spotting. On the whole they are strong-growing bulbs with glossy slender green foliage and widely spaced blooms of bright golden-lemon petals more or less recurved. There is usually a generous sprinkling of small almost black spots. Better stems carry up to three dozen flowers. It is a strain introduced by Jan de Graaff from Oregon in 1958. Lime tolerant. 1.2–1.8 m (4–6 ft) high.

'DISCOVERY'

A sister seedling to 'Pirate' but totally distinct. Long buds of soft whispered colours, silver and pale blush pinks, opening to show recurved tips of rich reddish lilac but shading to lilac-pink and to a very pale centre. Dotted crimson. Lime tolerant. 90 cm–1.2 m (3–4 ft) high.

'HORNBACK'S GOLD'

Strong 1.2 m (4 ft) stems holding several largish, impressive hanging blooms of rich glowing yellow only lightly spotted. Wide petals sweeping out and curving back. Thick smooth texture. Lime tolerant.

'LADY BOWES LYON'

A classically formed lily in rich shining dark red ornamented with neat black spots. The spacing of the blooms in pyramids helps emphasize the wide form of the individual flower with petals sweeping widely outwards and then recurving. Mid summer, 90cm–1.2m (3–4ft) high.

'LANGTRY'

Less tall than most at 90cm (3ft) and looking a picture of health with dark stems and leaves. Bright yellow flower colour is highlighted by the dark brown pollen and deep maroon spots. Gives bulbils. Flowers in mid summer. Avoid lime.

'MAXWILL'

Well over 50 years old but clean stock can still give a good show of perhaps two dozen or more bright scarlet-red flowers with spots. Well formed pyramids. Dark stems, narrow leaves, and growing from 1.2–2m (4–6ft) high. Early to mid summer. Lime tolerant.

'PEGGY NORTH'

Another of Dr North's *L. lankongense* hybrids, this one is pale orange with spotting. Avoid lime.

'ROSEMARY NORTH'

One of the intriguing pastel-coloured *L. lankongense* hybrids. Not too dominant warm shades of buff orange. 1.2–1.5m (4–5ft) high. Avoid lime with this lovely variety.

'THESEUS'

Richly coloured red hybrid with well spaced turkscap flowers. Strong plant with plenty of blooms, stems 1.5–2m (5–6ft) high. Has *L. lankongense* as grandparent and inherits the glorious scent.

DIVISION II. MARTAGON HYBRIDS

The important hybrids are those between *L. hansonii* and *L. martagon*. They are all very long-lived plants. Bulbs may be a bit tardy in their first year but once settled will increase year by year and make a very lovely sight in early and mid summer. Starting with groups of three, the varied shades are most intriguing. They are, of course, completely lime tolerant, and appear to be very resistant to virus. While petals of the pendant flowers all recurve, they do so much less strictly than those of *L. martagon*, giving a more relaxed and happy appearance to all, thanks to *L. hansonii*. Thanks also to the Backhouse team who bred many in the first decades of the century.

'DAIRY MAID'

Typical Backhouse Hybrid with lots of smallish turkscaps in creamy yellow peppered with spots in the centre. 1.2–1.8m (4–6ft) high.

× *dalhansonii*

This is the official name for all the hybrids between *L. martagon* and *L. hansonii*. The original was from the dark martagon form, *L. m. dalmaticum* × *L. hansonii*, producing chestnut-coloured flowers spotted yellow. 90cm–1.2m (3–4ft) high.

'EARLY BIRD'

A fine Backhouse Hybrid with soft yellow blooms suffused magenta-pink, especially in bud; open flowers are a paler old gold lightly dotted dark

Upper: 'Mont Blanc', one of the most useful
of the upward-facing hybrids.

Lower: 'Pirate', a spritely hybrid with
unusually well-lacquered petal surfaces.

Upper: *'Prominence' makes a sturdy plant with subtly coloured flowers.*

Lower: *'Rosita' is a dark Asiatic with good heads of attractively coloured blooms.*

maroon. One of the first to open in early summer. 1.2–1.8m (4–6ft) high.

'INDIAN CHIEF'
Almost a metallic flower with shining shades of copper and bronze marked with dashes and dots of red bordering black. It arose as a mutation from 'Marhan'. 1.2–1.8m (4–6ft) High.

'JACQUES S. DIJT'
Bred from the white *L. martagon album* crossed with *L. hansonii* and registered in 1950. It has typical martagon flowers in a pale creamy yellow, spotted purple. 1.5–1.8m (5–6ft) high.

'MARHAN'
From the same parents as the last but dating from 1891. It has lost none of its vigour and remains one of the best of garden lilies. Strong stems quickly reach 1.2–1.8m (4–6ft) with large whorls of foliage and splendid orange flowers distinctively spotted chocolate-red. Petals recurve.

'MRS R. O. BACKHOUSE'
Named after the raiser in 1921 and obtained from the reverse cross *L. hansonii* × *L. martagon*. Golden-yellow blooms teeter on the border of tangerine and are spotted red, while the buds are suffused a mauvey pink.

PAISLEY HYBRIDS
Raised in Oregon from *L. martagon album* crossed with *L. hansonii* but also involving Backhouse Hybrids. The series covers a spectrum from palish yellows through to oranges and dark shades, some almost mahogany, and pale purples. 90cm–1.8m (3–6ft) high.

'SHANTUNG'
A pink mauve selection from the Backhouse series, a pleasing warm colour with little dots. Strong tall plant. 1.5–2m (5–7ft) high.

'SUTTON COURT'
Named after the Backhouse home, a creamy straw-yellow one with a few spots. Petals do not recurve so much as the martagon, making it look more effective. Buds and the outsides of the petals are flushed mauve. 1.2–1.8m (4–6ft) high.

'W. O. BACKHOUSE'
Showing perhaps more of the *L. hansonii* habit than some and coloured a warm orange, made to seem more intense by the generous application of chocolate spots. 1.2–1.8m (4–6ft) high.

DIVISION III. CANDIDUM HYBRIDS

× *testaceum*
This is a famous accidental hybrid dating back to the beginning of the 1800s, a seedling from *L. candidum* × *L. chalcedonicum*. More or less pendant blooms are a most pleasing soft peachy salmon shade of orange. The flowers are large and wide, taking after the Madonna lily but petals, after making a wide sweep, gently curl back. It inevitably became virused but there is now fresh stock that has benefited from a laboratory clean-up and micropropagation. Completely lime tolerant. Early and mid summer, 1.2–1.5m (4–5ft) high.

DIVISION IV. AMERICAN HYBRIDS

These are all characterized by the whorled leaves, strong upright habit, pendant flower pose and petals recurving to greater or lesser extent. They are tolerant of wide ranges of soil. They exhibit a remarkable resistance to virus. At their best in mid summer.

BELLINGHAM HYBRIDS

These were raised in America originally around 1918 and involved several of the wild American species, in particular *L. pardalinum*, *L. ocellatum* and *L. parryi*. They are sometimes offered as a mix under this name but one or two clones were selected and continue to be offered separately, 'Shuksan' and 'Buttercup' being two. Other species then became involved in the breeding: these included *L. bolanderi* and *L. kelloggii*. 90 cm–2 m (3–7 ft) high.

BULLWOOD HYBRIDS

These were bred in England by Mr Derek Fox from *L. pardalinum* by pollen of a pink American species hybrid. The result was a most happy series of strong plants with large pendant flowers in colours ranging from warm apricot through pinky oranges to red and particularly dark cherry shades. Most are two-toned, white or golden petal bases being finished off with richer shades towards the tips. They stand well and hold their flowers gracefully. Petals sweep gently back and point upwards rather than curling into balls. Mid summer, 1.5–2.4 m (5–8 ft) high.

'BUTTERCUP'

Rich golden wide recurved flowers glowing strongly and very happily freckled with conspicuous spots. A Bellingham Hybrid 90 cm–1.5 m (3–5 ft) high.

'CHERRYWOOD'

This is a clone selected from the Bullwood Hybrids. Pendant blooms are beautifully hung out, each highly lacquered and vivid in its dominant rich cherry-red but with a pleasing golden-spotted centre. It is the clean lines of the flowers that emphasize the quality: sharply cut petals make lovely curved lines to end pointing up and out. 1.8–2.4 m (6–8 ft) high.

'DAIRY MAID'

A name also used for a Martagon Hybrid, so be careful. It was named in 1947 and came from a *L. pardalinum* × *L. parryi* seedling on which *L. parryi* pollen was used. The result is a tangerine lily with well reflexed petals that have a light peppering of spots, 1.2–1.8 m (4–6 ft) high.

'LAKE TAHOE'

A distinctive hybrid with a pale, almost white centre, green at the base but banded gold and dotted crimson. The upper half of the long tapering recurving petals is a deep cherry red. 1.8–2.4 m (6–8 ft) high.

'LAKE TULARE'

Many blooms hung out on long angled flower stalks. A rich glowing maroon-red gives way to a pale near-white base but with gold banding and crimson dots. Petals curve round to point upwards. 1.8–2.4 m (6–8 ft) high.

'PEACHWOOD'
A clone selected from the Bullwood Hybrids. Lovely soft peach-coloured and spotted recurved flowers that are best in semi-shade where the sun cannot fade them. 1.8–2.4 m (6–8 ft) high.

'ROSEWOOD'
Another Bullwood Hybrid. This one has good-sized flowers with long pointed petals sweeping wide and then upwards with their bases pale and spotted but gently shading to a full glowing pink. 1.8–2 m (6–7 ft) high.

'SHUKSAN'
A Bellingham Hybrid from *L. humboldtii* × *L. pardalinum*, named in 1933 and still going strong. Lots of well

Above: 'Sterling Star' is one of the easiest Asiatic Hybrids for the garden or cutting. Opposite: 'Corsage' produces no pollen so can be worn on clothing without staining.

recurved rounded flowers of rich old gold tipped with crimson. Gently spotted. 1.2–1.8 m (4–6 ft) high.

DIVISION VI. TRUMPET HYBRIDS

These perfumed hybrids are the result of interbreeding several species, such as *L. regale*, *sulphureum*, *sargentiae*, *brownii* and *leucanthum*. They are strong growers enjoying deep humus enriched soils and able to grow with lime.

'AFRICAN QUEEN'

Large widely flared trumpets that are a rich golden tangerine inside. On the exterior of the outer three petals and along the edges of the inner ones the colouring is a red-brown that helps to intensify the overall glowing effect. Strong stems 1.2–1.5 m (4–5 ft) high carry several heads. A dozen blooms easily achieved. Mid summer.

'BLACK DRAGON'

Large long buds of dark purple-red open to show off dazzling white interiors. 1.2–1.5 m (4–5 ft) high.

GOLDEN CLARION STRAIN

Trumpet-type flowers, the precursors of 'Golden Splendour'. Strong growing; lime tolerant. Height 1–1.2 m (3–4 ft).

GOLDEN SPLENDOUR

Series of richly gilded trumpets that open wide to display their riches. The backs of the outer petals are a well matured burgundy, as are the sides of the inner ones. These strong plants are the most readily available of the golden trumpet kinds. They stand 1.2–1.5 m (4–5 ft) high.

'GREEN DRAGON'

A clone selected originally from the Olympic Hybrids, with beautiful white interiors and a lovely chartreuse exterior. 1.2–2 m (4–7 ft) high.

GREEN MAGIC

This is a series of plants of similar parentage owing much to the fine species *L. sargentiae*. Typical flowers are large trumpets of glistening white with possibly a green-shaded base and maybe flushed green on the outside. 90 cm–1.8 m (3–6 ft) high.

'LIMELIGHT'

Well-loved selection from the more greeny yellow trumpets. This has long trumpets that open widely at the mouth and are a cool limy yellow, a shade that seems to hold better in semi-shade. Established bulbs can manage a lot of flowers on stems reaching 1.5–2 m (5–7 ft) high.

'MOONLIGHT'

There is an orange Asiatic clone called, somewhat inappropriately, 'Moonlight'. Here we are dealing with a strain of lilies characterized by buds that are usually green and flowers more or less deeply painted in tones of cool greeny yellow. 1.2–1.5 m (4–5 ft) high.

OLYMPIC HYBRIDS

This strain is of traditionally trumpet-shaped flowers usually pure white but possibly shaded green on the outside. When first marketed it included clones with pale yellow and pink tinted flowers and wine-coloured buds. 1.2–1.5 m (4–5 ft) high.

PINK PERFECTION

Originally there was a fair diversity of plants in this series, some being relatively light coloured pinks, but now the dominant clones are coloured dark maroon-pink, described rather unkindly by some as beetroot pink. They are impressive plants and flowers. I have had stems up to 2 m (7 ft) with over 30 huge blooms loading the surrounding air with perfume and striking awe into onlookers by their magnificent size and rich colours. 1.5–2 m (5–7 ft) high.

SUNBURST TYPES

When the trumpets were being bred on the Oregon Bulb Farms the Asiatic species *L. henryi* was brought into play. By crossing this with a number of selected forms of trumpet species, quite amazing crops of seeds were sown and plants raised. Collectively they were known as Aurelians. Some under the influence of *L. henryi* broke away from the trumpet form and were wide star shapes. These were marketed as Sunburst types such as 'Bright Star':

'BRIGHT STAR'

This grows in much the same way as *L. henryi*, stems reaching up and then arching. White petals reach out and recurve a bit; in the centre the petals are stained with honey orange. Good plants may reach 1.8 m (6 ft) high with up to a dozen or more flowers in mid and late summer.

DIVISION VII. ORIENTAL HYBRIDS

These are mainly the result of hybridizing the two species, *L. auratum* and *L. speciosum*. Heavily scented. Avid lime haters.

'BLACK BEAUTY'

Hybrid from *L. speciosum rubrum* × *L. henryi*. It has much of the *L. speciosum* form and flowers of very dark red with only the petal margins white and the very centre green. Strong. Mid summer, 90 cm–1.8 m (3–6 ft) high.

'CASABLANCA'

Hugely impressive with 20–25 cm (8–10 in) wide snowy white flowers of very shallow bowl shape with firm wide petals. Late summer and early autumn, 75 cm–1.2 m (30 in–4 ft) high.

'DOMINIQUE'

Dwarfish, growing only 30–45 cm (12–18 in) high but having large rich crimson flowers stippled a darker shade in the middle and with a small green nectary furrow in the very centre. Late summer.

IMPERIAL CRIMSON

A strain with 1.2–1.5 m (4–5 ft) stems and wide flat flowers of rich crimson with white margins. Late summer.

IMPERIAL GOLD

Strain of huge white flowers with a broad band of gold down the centre of each petal and spotted crimson. Late summer. 1.5 m (5 ft) high.

IMPERIAL SILVER

Strain characterized by flat pure white flowers with wide petals and quantities of tiny crimson spots. Late summer, 1.2–1.5 m (4–5 ft) high.

'JOURNEY'S END'

Several large rich crimson-pink flowers, darker in a line down the centre of each petal but fading to white at the edges and petal tips. Wide flowers with petals very gently recurved. Spotted darker. Late summer, 1.5 m (5 ft) high.

'STARGAZER'

Large upward-facing flowers of very rich crimson. Edges of petals are a pinky red and dotted darker shades towards the centre. Standing 1.2–1.5 m (4–5 ft) and blooming several weeks earlier than most in mid summer.

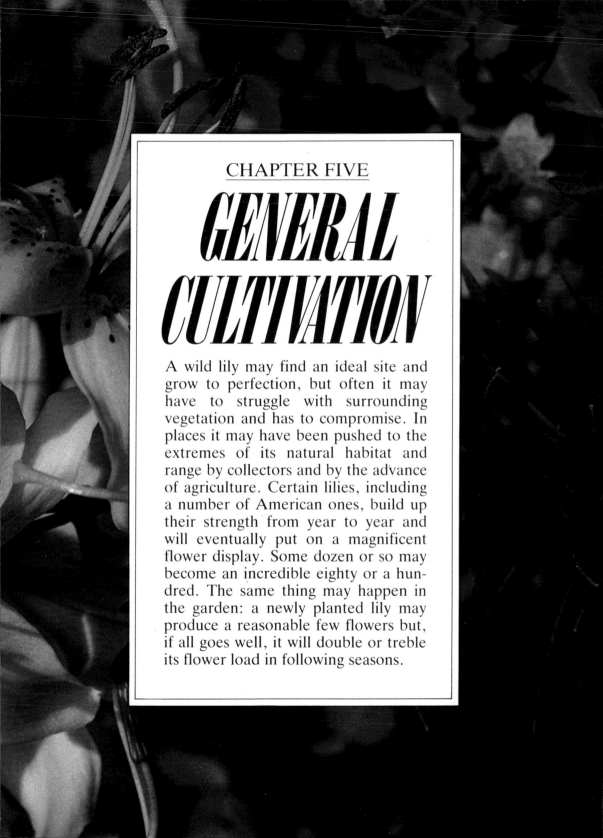

CHAPTER FIVE

GENERAL CULTIVATION

A wild lily may find an ideal site and grow to perfection, but often it may have to struggle with surrounding vegetation and has to compromise. In places it may have been pushed to the extremes of its natural habitat and range by collectors and by the advance of agriculture. Certain lilies, including a number of American ones, build up their strength from year to year and will eventually put on a magnificent flower display. Some dozen or so may become an incredible eighty or a hundred. The same thing may happen in the garden: a newly planted lily may produce a reasonable few flowers but, if all goes well, it will double or treble its flower load in following seasons.

NATURAL SITES

As a generalization, a wild species transferred to the pampered role of a garden lily will reveal its full potential, becoming a stouter plant altogether and more floriferous. On the other hand some wild ones are so closely adapted to their precise natural conditions that the gardener may struggle to please them.

Most hybrids, including all those most often seen for sale, are much easier to grow than many species. Their mixed parentage has helped overcome some of the parent's inhibitions; they seem to own a hybrid vigour that gives them a head start whether grown in pots or in the garden outside.

Wild lilies are usually found in fairly deep soils on mountain sides and sloping meadows where they enjoy free drainage of cold air as well as moisture which is plentiful underground in the growing months. Often in winter the bulbs are insulated from very sodden conditions by deep blankets of snow which stay in position for several months.

GARDEN SITES

We are not likely to be able to provide an exact copy of the native environment and climate for our species. The best sites are going to provide good drainage and are not going to be too water laden in winter. Drainage and soil content can be improved by arranging built up beds, borders, or areas where the added soil can be enriched with humus; by being some inches above the general level, the site will always be well drained.

Obviously we do not wish our lilies to be liable to drought but the plants are better adapted to periods of water shortage than to constant stagnant moisture. In the wild some species grow in areas where they may be without rain for several weeks and even months.

Lilies enjoy shade for their bulbs, but like to grow into fresh air and sunshine. Good air drainage will help to prevent frost damage; it will also help prevent fungus diseases getting a foothold. Dark, still, wet spots are the likeliest venues for fungus troubles.

Growing lilies between shrubs has several advantages. The shrubs provide shade for the bulbs and roots. They also give shelter from frost and wind. Hard late frosts can sometimes be damaging to lilies, such as *L. regale*, that have got into vigorous early growth. Shrubs can also give the support that some lilies enjoy.

There is no need to deny oneself the pleasure of growing lilies in places where the sun does not reach or makes only a fleeting appearance, provided the position is not terribly dark. I have grown some interesting species and hybrids in this way. However, here we should advocate the ideal. There is no better time than now to begin to grow lilies as the choice is wider than ever. Today's hybrids are basically of such easy culture that they will often manage magnificently even when conditions are far from ideal.

There is absolutely no excuse these days why every gardener should not grow lilies for there are hybrids suited to every possible situation.

SOILS

Lilies enjoy the good life: they like deep soils rich in humus. Textural structure of the soil is important. To grow freely and give of their best in bloom and in increasing growth, the bulbs like an open friable soil with air, grit and humus. Many kinds not only have an extensive rooting system from the bulb but produce roots from that portion of the stem below ground. Stem rooting does two jobs. It anchors the stem firmly in the soil, but it also provides feeding that is often not just an auxiliary supply but an essential element in the battle for survival. Magnificent flowering stems of *L. auratum* and other lilies have been found, when dug up after blooming, to have been almost wholly dependent on the stem roots as the bulbs had disintegrated. The soil structure and content above the bulbs is as important as below. The value of mulches is difficult to over-emphasize.

□ACIDITY AND ALKALINITY: pH VALUES

After drainage the prime factor in considering soils for lilies is their acidity or alkalinity, conveniently measured in pH levels, 7 being neutral with lower numbers signalling progressively greater acidity and with numbers above 7 showing increasing alkalinity. Many wild lilies prefer neutral or acid soils; for some, like *L. speciosum* and *L. auratum*, lime is a deadly poison. However, there is a reasonable number of species tolerant of lime even if not exactly enthusiastic about it.

Many hybrids are far more tolerant of lime than their ancestor species. Therefore having a somewhat alkaline soil is no bar to growing a wide selection. It is sensible to repeat the advice that it is best to go with nature rather than try to make major changes in the environmental factors. Physical features such as shelter and drainage can be changed; chemical changes to the soil are more difficult and long-term undertakings.

The list given below is of kinds that may be available for sale which are oblivious to the presence of lime or may even enjoy it, together with others that, like the youngster faced with spinach on the dinner plate, makes the best of a less than inviting job.

L. candidum	*L. monadelphum*
L. cernuum	*L. pardalinum*
L. chalcedonicum	*L. pomponium*
L. concolor	*L. pyrenaicum*
L. davidii	*L. regale*
L. hansonii	*L. szovitsianum*
L. henryi	Martagon Hybrids
L. longiflorum	Asiatic Hybrids
L. martagon	Trumpet Hybrids

As the hybrids listed cover a large number of cultivars, the available types for soils with some lime is really impressive.

Acidity or alkalinity levels are not all that easy to change. Within a small area much may be done for a while but the influence of the fundamental surrounding soil is going to be the major force in the eventual outcome. To change the reading of a garden soil by one pH unit

Above: 'Barbara North' is one of an elegant group of lilies bred by Dr North.

Opposite: Citronella Strain is a notably vigorous, colourful, easily-grown strain.

requires a huge effort. Peats are acid materials but it would need massive loads of these incorporated into a sub-urban garden to materially alter the pH level. It is always worth adding peat or humus rich materials to all soils, except those already laden with peat; every handful helps the structure of the soil and starts to counteract any alkalinity. Continual mulching with leaf mould, compost and peat continues the process. The greater the volume of humus in the soil the greater will be the tolerance of highish pH levels. The additions of chemicals can help but are probably best viewed as auxiliary rather than mainline remedies.

Flowers of sulphur incorporated into the top few centimetres of soil at the rate of no more than $150 g/m^2$ (4oz/sq yd) will help. This may be repeated twice a year on sandy soils but would otherwise be an annual application until the de-sired pH level is achieved. On heavy clay soils the effect of flowers of sulphur is to work against the flocculation pro-cesses and so cause additional problems. Sequestrene may be thought another possible form of chemical manipulation. However, it is dangerous applied to the foliage and not all that effective in uncontrolled open soil conditions.

Very chalky or alkaline soils are going to suit a few lilies including notably the Martagons and their hybrids. Beds built up with bricks, logs or other walls may be filled with predominantly peaty or leaf mould soils. With chemical warfare detailed above it is possible to provide over the alkaline base a home for some of those not happy with very alkaline soils. Gardeners with very limy soils, if they feel they must grow the real lime haters, are best advised either to grow them in large pots or to move house and garden.

□PREPARING THE SOIL

Clumps of the Madonna lily, *L. candi-dum*, seem to flourish on neglect in cottage gardens. You may try neglect with your Madonnas and other lilies and find it an unprofitable enterprise. Cot-tage garden lilies probably do well because they are the survivors suited to the soils and are growing in an environ-ment free from the diseases other lilies may bring. In effect they are quaran-tined.

A few kinds grow well in uninviting soils. *L. pardalinum* and *L. p. gigan-teum* will often manage with little trouble on heavy wet clays, the very opposite to what is recommended for the majority. *L. martagon* will natural-ize in many gardens given the chance and seems to flourish in a variety of unimproved soils.

With those short words of comfort to those unenthusiastic about gardening labour we move to the real truth of the matter. The vast majority of lilies enjoy deep well worked soil and will amply repay the extra attention given to soil preparation and maintenance. Some ini-tial work may suffice for a long period of time. We should really adopt the atti-tude of growing soil rather than growing plants.

Ideally the site chosen for a group of lilies should be dug thoroughly, prefer-ably well beyond a spit deep, and if the drainage seems poor, then another site should be chosen or drainage arranged away from the site. Land drain pipes can be laid to lower ground. The addition of home-made compost in the lower soil will help to improve its structure. The most important part of the soil to improve is going to be the top spit, roughly the first 25 cm (10 in). If a group of three to ten bulbs is to be planted it may be possible to remove this top spit, dig over the lower soil incorporating some humus material and bring the level to about 20–15 cm (8–6 in) deep. Large bulbs are going to need a hole at least 20 cm (8 in) deep to ensure at least 10 cm (4 in) of soil over their noses. This is a basic minimum for most lilies. There are some with small bulbs and these may suffice with a little less, but it is better to be a little deep than too shallow. *L. candidum* is the exception: it should be planted with noses scarcely covered.

The topsoil returned over the planted bulbs should be mixed with plenty of humus material like leaf mould or peat, in quantities of up to half the total volume. A layer of grit or sharp sand under the bulbs does nothing for drainage, but the roots do seem to enjoy grit in their soil, almost like a good fibre diet.

PLANTING

Bulbs are probably best planted with twice their own depth of soil over their noses. Distances apart will vary according to the character of the plant and with some consideration of future plans. Those that are to be planted permanent-

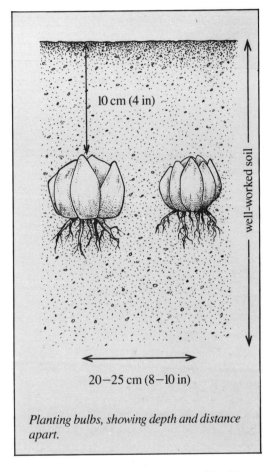

10 cm (4 in)

well-worked soil

20–25 cm (8–10 in)

Planting bulbs, showing depth and distance apart.

ly should be given at least 30–40 cm (12–15 in) spacing; *L. pardalinum* and *L. martagon* will soon make this territory their own. They need space to flex their muscles. A group of Asiatic Hybrids which you know are going to be lifted after a couple of years to be split and moved on, can be grown at closer density, perhaps with only 10 cm (4 in) between bulbs. Usually a 15 cm (6 in) spacing between bulbs will be a minimum.

'Discovery' is here growing happily in one of the author's garden beds.

Lilium 'Marhan' is still one of the best of the L. martagon × L. hansonii hybrids.

Planting is best done in early autumn. If you have your own bulbs or can get your supplier to hand over bulbs at this time, all well and good. You stand a good chance of the bulbs establishing a healthy root system before the onset of the winter.

Bulbs that are flourishing in the garden are probably best left alone, but there comes a time when they may be getting overcrowded or when surrounding shrubs have encroached too enthusiastically over the lilies. Then the best time to move the bulbs will be a few weeks after flowering, perhaps four weeks later. The whole plant can be carefully lifted. Soil can be gently worked away from the stem below what was formerly soil level to see whether there are any small bulbs or bulbils to be removed for growing on. Healthy masses of large bulbs will need teasing carefully apart. Then all the bulbs need replanting without delay in a prepared spot. Having been firmed in, half the flower stem can be removed. This will allow the plant the majority of the leaves but will reduce the chance of the wind rocking the stem and causing problems.

Whilst it may be possible to get bulbs from trade sources in the autumn, most firms will not supply until the early spring. What happens is that as the various lilies reach their harvest time, the bulbs are lifted, cleaned and put into cold storage. From the trader's point of view this is the sensible procedure. The different types of lilies become ready to lift over a long period; by storing them an order may be sent out with all the different kinds all in one go. This is easily the most economical method. Bulbs are normally sent to gardeners in the late winter or early spring. Later orders may be sent in mid spring and showcases of bulbs will be seen from autumn until late spring.

Spring delivery is not all that much of a handicap. The soil is warming and the new roots are soon made and encouraged to expand rapidly to support the quickly growing stems. If bulbs are received in the late winter when the ground is wet or frozen and gardening is impossible, they may be either stored in damp peat in a cool spot or planted in pots in a cool greenhouse or conservatory. They can be planted out later when the weather is more conducive to growth, health and happiness. The whole pot load should be planted out with as little disturbance as possible.

SUPPORTS

Many lilies need no support. There are two main arguments in favour of support for some lilies. First, heavy flower heads in more exposed sites are saved from the worst effects of strong winds which could rock the whole plant and damage it. Stakes placed in position at the time of planting can help to mark the bulbs' site and so safeguard them before above ground growth is made. Clumps of lilies can be surrounded by a ring of chicken wire to a height of 60 cm (2 ft). This fulfils the second argument, the idea of this support usually being to prevent marauding rabbits eating their fill of the bulbs and shoots. It does not

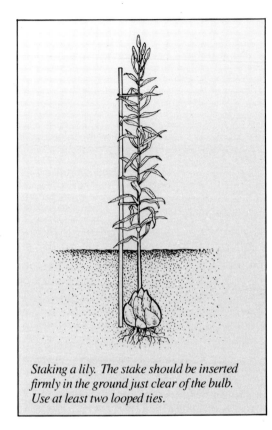

Staking a lily. The stake should be inserted firmly in the ground just clear of the bulb. Use at least two looped ties.

sound the last word in gardening aesthetics but it is practical and in a surprisingly short time the wire disappears amidst the foliar dress of the lilies and their neighbours.

If one is staking a lily it should be done thoroughly. The cane is supposed to hold the lily firm, not the other way round. Stout canes rammed hard into the ground at planting time need to be sufficiently strong and firm to hold the weight of a stem, say of 'Pink Perfection', that could be well over 2 m (6 ft) high with over two dozen large flowers at the top. In a strong wind it could be a

considerable load. In open sites it is the trumpets and the large oriental types like *L. auratum* and its hybrids that are most likely to need stakes. Asiatic Hybrids are unlikely to need such aid and comfort except as anti-rabbit protection.

MULCHING AND FEEDING

Lilies revel in mulches. They enjoy the insulating layer over their roots as well as the fresh root run for the stem roots and the extra feed that is going to be provided. Pure peat mulches are useful but lack nourishment. Leaf mould is much more beneficial. Well made compost is going to be a very worthwhile addition to the soil around the lilies. Different materials can be mixed and a sprinkling of general fertilizer added at the same time. Tomato fertilizers high in potash are useful for lilies. Even a mulch of pulverized bark is helpful. It will certainly keep weeds down, keep the soil cool, help retain moisture and, as it decomposes, add to the acidity of the whole.

If you can manage more than one mulch, one in late spring and another in mid summer will do a world of good. These could be the periods when a feed is given. The type of fertilizer to pick is likely to be one from those recommended for tomatoes or potatoes, often higher in potash and phosphorus than nitrogen. By law the formula of a fertilizer offered for sale must be printed on the pack. This is done simply as proportions of the main elements, nitrogen (N), phosphorus (P), and

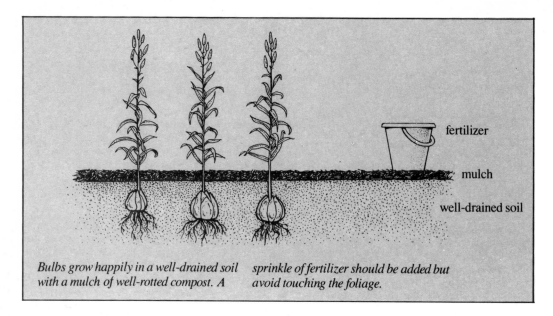

Bulbs grow happily in a well-drained soil with a mulch of well-rotted compost. A sprinkle of fertilizer should be added but avoid touching the foliage.

potassium (K). For instance the formula printed on some packs is NPK 7-7-7.

A tomato or potato fertilizer might be NPK 5-10-10. As the first number refers to nitrogen (N) it will be seen that this is probably a better buy for the lilies than the 7-7-7 formula. Too much nitrogen encourages leaf growth and may result in sappy foliage and stems that invite troubles from fungi and insects. Dressings of 70 g/m² (2 oz/sq yd) are perfectly adequate. This is best applied to the ground and raked in lightly before the lily shoots appear, a job for early spring. The counsel of perfection will be to follow this with two further half doses in the late spring and mid summer. On these occasions the fertilizer should be distributed very carefully so that none touches the lily leaves or stems.

Wood ash, bonfire ash or the ash from a wood burning stove can be used with good results on all kinds of bulbs. Lilies certainly enjoy the potash. A word of warning: whilst this source of potash is almost worth its weight in gold, it must be used with care near rhododendrons and other lime haters as the ash is alkaline.

Where you may be using thick mulches of bark or sawdust as a very effective weed cover there will, however, be a requisitioning of the bacteria whose role in life is to break down such material. The practical effect is that the nitrogen that would otherwise have been made available by these nitrogen-fixing bacteria is temporarily out of stock. All the bacteria rush to the new material and get involved in the long job

Opposite: 'Sutton Court' is one of the L. martagon hybrids bred by Mrs Backhouse.

of breaking down this layer. Eventually equilibrium is reached, the mulch is broken down and the soil enriched, but, to start with, the temporary nitrogen starvation shows up in the paler foliage and slower growth. A dose of balanced general fertilizer may fit the bill. If sawdust is piled on thickly it may be good sense to incorporate with it some nitrogen in the form of sulphate of ammonia at $70 \, \text{g/m}^2$ (2 oz/sq yd).

WATERING

Lilies are not fond of having their leaves splashed with water and dirt. In many gardens they will never really need watering outside unless they are in a particularly dry spot or in a period of prolonged drought. Good soil structure and sensible mulching will maintain health and strength even in very dry periods. If you do decide that water is needed try to water the ground, not the lily, and make a thorough job of it. A dampening down is no good at all. A hose without a sprinkler should be allowed to soak the soil. Liquid fertilizers could be applied at such times or in place of solid feeds. Tomato fertilizers will again be adequate.

SAVING SEEDS

From the time the shoots pierce the soil surface until flowering time there seems plenty of incentive to take good care of the plants and the surrounds. Anticipation of the flowering effort encourages us to feed, to stake, to weed and generally fuss around. As the blooms fade away and petals fall the magnetic

pull lessens. It may not matter a great deal if we forget the clumps we were enjoying a few days or weeks ago, but possibly it might be good policy to cut away the flower head. Reducing the height of the stem appreciably lessens the liability to wind rocking and saves the plants wasting energy on seed production, whilst all the leaves are probably saved so that work goes on to build up strength for next year.

If you are planning to save seeds from a clump it may be a sensible idea to try harvesting the number of pods you think will be sufficient by only taking one pod from a stem; this may well be the first flower to open on the stem. The idea is to spread the load, but also to try to ensure that the plant has the best possible chance to ripen its seed. In poor summers ripening is not always easy, certainly not in the later flowering kinds. Therefore it makes sense to get the earliest flower on to the job as quickly as possible. Having only one pod to cope with does seem to hurry the ripening process.

WINTER CARE

Winter care is going to be mainly a matter of trying to ensure that the bulbs are not sitting in stagnant water. Hopefully our siting and soil preparation should deal with this. On occasion I have laid a sheet of polythene over a clump of lily species I thought would not appreciate a wet winter and anchored this down with a covering of shredded bark that made all look tidy as well. The sheet can be pulled away in the spring

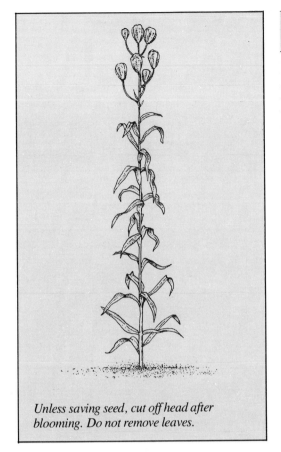

Unless saving seed, cut off head after blooming. Do not remove leaves.

GROWING LILIES IN CONTAINERS

Lilies are easy in containers with drainage. There are many advantages. Compost can exactly match the lily's needs. This means the ones that hate lime can be grown by gardeners whose soil may be as white as chalk. Bulbs of most cultivars can be encouraged very easily to bloom earlier, or even later, than the norm. Pots full of lilies just ready to bloom can be planted just where they are needed in the garden, or may be enjoyed on the patio, in the conservatory or inside the house. The few rather tender kinds, like the white trumpet *L. formosanum*, do beautifully in containers.

With the boom in conservatories in recent years there has evolved renewed interest in lilies in pots as they are marvellous subjects for cool conservatories.

Many gardeners enjoy growing all their lilies in pots and containers. They feel they have complete control of them and can enjoy them more intimately. Others with no garden at all but with a yard or patio only can still have a collection blooming for a long period. They are very amenable.

Most of the kinds grown outside will grow as well in containers. The martagons and the American species are the least successful; these would normally be better in the garden. All the many Asiatic Hybrids, the Trumpet Hybrids and the wonderful Oriental group would find pot culture sheer heaven. Some of many that are excellent include:

when the bulbs are beginning to get active again. Another autumn job in preparation for the winter is to ensure that there is no weed and rotting waste around. Slugs are a real pest: we need to make the site as unattractive as possible for them. I may be deceiving myself but I have the impression that scattered wood ash from the wood burning stove appears to keep slugs at bay, as well as doing good. Slugs do not seem to like moving over the rough surface which is created by ashes.

Asiatics	Trumpets	Orientals
L. 'Harmony'	L. regale	L. speciosum forms
L. 'Destiny'	L. 'African Queen'	L. auratum
L. 'Enchantment'	L. Pink Perfection	L. Imperial Silver
L. 'Rosita'	L. Golden Splendour	L. Imperial Crimson
L. 'Sunray'	L. 'Royal Gold'	L. Imperial Gold
L. 'Mont Blanc'	L. 'Limelight'	L. 'Stargazer'

Pots or other larger containers, earthenware or plastic, are going to be fine provided they have sufficient depth to give the bulb room for compost below and at least 10cm (4in) over their noses when planted. Drainage holes are imperative. Roots and bulbs will rot in containers without adequate drainage.

As a generalization, the larger the container the better the bulbs perform. Soil moisture and temperature are not going to fluctuate so erratically in larger ones. I have grown many thousands of Asiatics in pots as small as 13cm (5in). One bulb to a pot provided a good plant. However the advice is to use larger ones. Pots of 20cm (8in) will take single bulbs of large trumpet types; 25cm (10in) pots will house three bulbs. Tubs could be home for a dozen or more of any kind.

In troughs or tubs it is perfectly in order to leave bulbs in for more than one season. It used to be a regular routine to have kinds like L. regale grown in the same large container for a decade without lifting. Each season the top soil was removed and fresh added.

Bulbs may be potted in the autumn or spring. As bulbs are normally most readily available from late winter to early spring we shall assume planting at

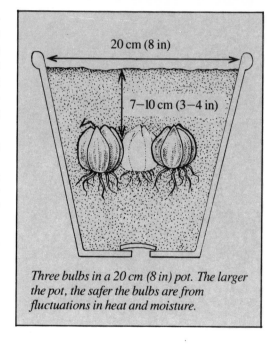

Three bulbs in a 20 cm (8 in) pot. The larger the pot, the safer the bulbs are from fluctuations in heat and moisture.

this time in the following suggested routine.

Compost should be an open airy mix. Many different composts are perfectly adequate. They should be neutral or slightly acid. Soil-based composts made without the addition of chalk will do well for most lilies. One of the main

Opposite: *Lilium 'Black Dragon' was introduced by Jan de Graaff in 1950.*

reasons for the less frequent appearance of these composts for sale is the difficulty of procuring good quality loam. Peat composts are very much easier to make up and are a more profitable item. Of the many that are on offer, those for ericaceous plants will be on the acid side of neutral and can be very successful, especially if made from coarse textured sphagnum moss peat. To be avoided are the dark powdery decomposed peats. All peat-based composts will be improved by adding some inert material like grit to keep them open in texture; this aids drainage. The proportion of grit to compost should be one part by volume of grit to three or four parts of compost.

I have used a variety of composts with good results. On occasion I have taken proprietary soil-based composts and added an equal volume of sphagnum peat. This added peat makes the mix rather more acid, it helps moisture retention, and makes it unlikely that it will become compacted and airless. Peat-based ones are very much lighter so that the pots are easy to move, but they are of course more easily blown over when plants are in full growth unless given extra support. A useful made up compost could be:

> 1 part sphagnum moss peat
> 1 part good garden loam
> 1 part sharp grit (parts by volume)
> (powdered tomato fertilizer can be added)

Perlite is a lightweight inert white material completely sterile and of neutral pH. It maintains its form and is a most useful replacement for grit and considerably helps the compost structure. It is relatively inexpensive and is easy to work with.

Bulbs should have 8–10cm (3–4 in) of compost over their noses. Depending on bulb size, 15–18cm (6–7in) pots will take a single bulb, 20–25cm (8–10in) ones may take one to six bulbs. Some species with small bulbs, like *L.pumilum* (*L.tenuifolium*), can be grown three to a 15cm (6in) pot. At the risk of being repetitious, I would emphasize the point that larger pots are easier to look after than small ones. Anyone with only a minimum of time available would be well advised to use as large a container as is practical.

Compost is placed in the bottom of the pot, the bulb or bulbs added and roots, if any, tucked into the compost. The remainder of the compost is added to cover the bulbs by 8–10cm (3–4in), leaving 1cm (½in) below the pot top for watering. They can be kept in a conservatory, greenhouse, or outside, free standing or in a plunge bed. To start with the pots may be crammed together. As the plants grow they can be given more room so that air circulates freely around at all times.

Initially the compost needs to be kept damp to encourage rooting. As the lilies get into more rapid growth and the weather becomes warmer the pots will need to be watched more closely because they are going to dry out much more quickly. Watering should not be done in too carefree a manner: lilies do not appreciate their leaves being spattered with water and dirt. This may cause physical and fungal damage. If pots are half sunk in peat they can take up much of their moisture from below; with large pots trickle irrigation is a possibility; otherwise pots standing on capillary matting will take some moisture from below but will need careful watering from above also.

Energetic bulbs can soon be looking for extra feed as they fill the pots with roots and begin to exhaust the limited feed in the compost. Ideal feeding will be a liquid one at 10-day intervals, using tomato or similar fertilizers. Light sprinklings of powdered or granular fertilizers can also be employed two or three times a season. All such fertilizers must not make direct contact with leaves or stems.

Bulbs of most types kept at a temperature of 15–16°C (60°F) will be ready to start blooming in 14 weeks.

If pots are moved to display points on the patio, or in a conservatory or living room, this is best done as the buds begin to colour. If the pots themselves can be shaded this will be helpful in keeping the bulbs and roots cooler. Pots outside will have their rate of transpiration accelerated and will dry out quickly. Lilies are remarkably resilient to drought but they are not cacti and should not be allowed to dry out. They do not want to be sitting in water so do not be tempted to place them in a container without drainage where a rainy period is going to drown them.

Trumpet and Oriental kinds can be most impressive in bloom, 1.5–2.5 m (5–8 ft) high. With many large blooms

open they can catch the wind as easily as a windjammer's sails. Heavy containers are going to be safer. They will be best well anchored in a position sheltered from the worst of any sudden gale.

After blooming, the flowering tops may be cut away. Bulbs should still be watered and fed. When the tops die down in the autumn, the bulbs can be turned out and repotted. Alternatively the bulbs can be left in the pots and only the top soil replaced. Compost can be removed down to the level of the bulb, something that may be easier to manage in larger containers than in small pots thoroughly filled with roots. Pots can be overwintered out of extreme frost and where they will not be sodden with rain all the time.

PESTS

The most obvious pests of lilies are rabbits and slugs. As their numbers increase rabbits are becoming a major pest again in the more rural areas. They are especially annoying early in the year when they seem to enjoy nibbling all types of new growth. Obviously the best plan is to keep them out of the garden completely. The cost of installing rabbit-proof wiring around the garden may seem prohibitive at first glance. Over a period of a relatively few years it could well prove a very good investment. If you decide to try to live with free-range rabbits then clumps of lilies can be protected by rings of chicken wire 60–75 cm (2–2½ ft) high. They look obtrusive to start with but foliage soon more or less hides them.

Slugs must have a place in the great plan of creation, but in the garden they seem an unmitigated scourge. Those that work on the surface can be dealt with relatively easily. Normal baiting will soon reduce the population to nil or manageable proportions. It is the smaller types that work just below the soil surface that are the most annoying. Clean cultivation and slug baits will help to keep them in check.

Slugs are at their most voracious and damaging when the bulbs have just

Above: *Golden Clarion is a fine example of a series that was named in 1948.*
Opposite: *Golden Splendour strain is a popular series of golden trumpet hybrids.*

started into growth and are sending their fresh shoots towards the surface. A few minutes nibbling at this stage destroys the flowering of the bulb for the year. Cleaning up in the autumn to try to ensure that there is no obvious banquet for slugs left around is the first step. Eliminating all weed growth and

keeping the surface clean will make the habitat less attractive to them. I believe that a scattering of wood ash worked into the top couple of centimetres or so of soil seems to deter the little beasties. The most important time for baiting is going to be the late winter into spring just before the bulbs get into active growth.

□ LILY BEETLE (*Lilioceris lilii*)

This pest is not a universal one, but where it is present it can be devastating in its effects. Both the larva and adult beetle eat off the leaves and can reduce plants to a wretched denuded mess, usually eating the juicy bits of the leaves and leaving the veins. (In Britain the pest is at present confined to the warmer counties of southern England, particularly Surrey, Suffolk and Hampshire.)

The beetle is bright orange scarlet with a black head. It is about 6–8mm (¼in) long. Larvae are a grubby yellow colour with dark heads and legs. They grow to 8–10mm (¼–⅜in) long when fully developed. When mature these larvae pupate in the soil. Any seen on lilies should be immediately destroyed. Where there is any likelihood of an infestation, the lilies can be sprayed with a systemic insecticide. Malathion will kill beetles and larvae. Early action is obviously best.

□ APHIDS

Aphids seem to attack most living plants, and the lily is no exception, although it may not be one of the most favoured by these pests. The most important reason for not encouraging aphids around your lilies is that they are often carriers of virus diseases. As they suck sap from the plant they can inject the tissue with one or more viruses that they have picked up elsewhere. Large numbers of aphids attacking the crowded flower buds can cause distortion and the abortion of some flowers. Systemic or contact insecticides will deal with these easily. Under glass the worst may be the melon aphid (*Aphis gossypii*). Among those that can also attack outdoor lilies will be the potato aphid (*Macrosiphum solanifolii*) and the peach aphid (*Myzus persicae*).

DISEASES

□ VIRUS DISEASES

These are probably the most important maladies of lilies. Prevention is better than cure for the simple reason that there is no cure once infected. It is a somewhat intricate subject as the same virus will often have a different effect on different types of lilies. Some lilies seem inherently resistant to viruses, others can manage quite a long life not too badly disabled by infection, but others will be rapidly reduced to worthless distressing twisted growth. *L. formosanum* and *L. longiflorum* are particularly vulnerable to viruses and once attacked show distinct symptoms quickly. Because of this they have often been used as indicator plants to check for virus. On the other hand some of the American species like *L. pardalinum* and others like *L. hansonii* and *L. davidii* seem to have a very high degree of immunity.

The most frequent symptom is going

to be a mottled appearance of the foliage. Such plants should be destroyed before they pass the trouble on to others. As viruses are normally passed by sap-sucking insects like aphids, it will make a considerable difference if groups of lilies are grown as separately from each other as possible. Shrubs in between will help to isolate the lilies. The gardener may think the shrubs a poor barrier but they can be surprisingly effective.

CUCUMBER MOSAIC VIRUS

This is a fairly common virus. When it attacks *L. formosanum* it reduces it quickly to ruin. Leaves become clearly streaked and then twisted before losing much of their life and turning into brittle waste. Stems too will become distorted. The same virus attacking more tolerant kinds is still going to produce yellow streaked foliage which will reduce the effectiveness of the plants. You will have to be resolute and destroy any infected plant.

LILY MOTTLE VIRUS

Attacked leaves become mottled or streaked with paler colour. The plant begins to have a poorly appearance and will eventually waste away. This debilitating effect may take longer to effect death in some kinds than others, but all the time it is a source of infection. This same virus is the one that causes the breaking of the colour in broken tulips; if you should grow these then they must obviously be as far away as possible from the lilies because they are still in growth when the lilies start to rocket upwards.

LILY SYMPTOMLESS VIRUS

This is a real problem as we cannot immediately see the effects. The plants rather slowly lose their vitality and eventually fade away. Attacks on the Asiatics, especially those with *L. davidii* and *L. lancifolium* (*tigrinum*) blood, are very difficult to diagnose as these lilies have a higher than usual degree of tolerance.

As is often the case, plants will succumb much more quickly when this virus is present with another. It may be present with another virus found in the well known 'Enchantment', called brown ring virus which can be recognized in the bulbs by the shorter scales held more loosely. Brown rings can be seen. Plants in growth are clearly not normal; they are paler, dwarfer and lacking in their usual debonair appearance.

□ BOTRYTIS (*Botrytis elliptica*)

This is not usually a very worrying disease. Plants growing in airy healthy conditions are unlikely to be affected. More vulnerable kinds like the Madonna lily may be affected in the spring in a period when the weather is still, moist and humid. You may notice the lower leaves collapsing and shrivelling. Severe attacks if not checked will defoliate a plant making it look grotesque.

Fungicide sprays will forestall any trouble and will help check it, if caught in its early stages. Commercial growers who have huge numbers growing in close proximity will spray regularly as a matter of course. They are likely to use freshly made Bordeaux mixture, still

Pink Perfection is one of the series of pink trumpets nowadays mainly in dark shades.

Imperial Crimson is the richest coloured of the three Imperial series.

one of the most effective of fungicides. Using plastic or other non-metallic containers, the mix is made as follows: 50 g of hydrated lime is worked into a thin paste and then stirred into 5 litres of water (1½oz/gal). The same quantity of copper sulphate is dissolved into 2.5 litres (½ gal) of warm water. When fully dissolved this is added to the lime solution whilst stirring vigorously. The mix is ready for spraying on to all the leaves, top and bottom sides and on to the stems. Surplus spray must be disposed of as it does not keep.

DISORDERS

Reading the rest of this section of the chapter may suggest that lilies are subject to all sorts of perils and cannot be long for this world. This is not the true picture. They can be marvellously trouble-free plants, very amply repaying any trouble taken for their care. Like the rest of vegetable creation they can suffer from drought and drowning. Drought they will withstand far better than most plants. In the wild many will have been used to going without rainfall for long periods. Below ground they may have adequate moisture to last them for months. On mountain sides there may well be moisture moving below ground to sustain them when above looks close to a desert. In well dug garden soils lilies will take a long time before they show any flagging as a symptom of their thirsty distress. Should they need watering, one real soaking of the ground will do more good than any number of sprinklings. As mentioned before, the water should be kept off the foliage.

Excess wet can be a more likely problem. This is especially the case in the long months through the winter and early spring. It is as well to plant the bulbs in places where they will not be sitting in constant water. In gardens with poor drainage it is worthwhile building up the soil levels of beds where lilies grow so that they are given some extra aid.

Occasionally an aberrant stem may appear flattened and possibly with more leaves and flowers than normal. Such fasciated stems are usually the result of exceptional growing conditions during a particularly vulnerable time, perhaps when the previous year's bulb was busy trying to split into two bulbs and forming embryo flower buds. Such freak stems will not be repeated the following year.

DIAGNOSIS

No growth above ground. This could be due to slugs eating through the stems below ground shortly after they have emerged from the bulb. Other soil pests include wireworm, leatherjackets and millipedes but these are unlikely to be present in such numbers as to constitute a major menace. Rabbits are an increasing problem and are always hungry. They will eat lilies at any time but especially as they emerge in the spring. Rings of wire netting around clumps may be necessary where bunnies abound. Growth soon obscures much of the netting.

Leaves wither and die on stem. Usually due to the fungus, *Botrytis elliptica,* which will be most likely to attack where plants are growing in crowded, airless spots where leaves are likely to be moist and conditions humid. Lilies like shade at the toes but enjoy plenty of air above.

Leaves become striped, mottled or distorted. Usually the result of virus infection. See above.

Leaf colour changes. From normal green to purple may indicate that the lot of the bulb below ground is not a happy one, it could be losing or have lost its roots due to rotting in excessive wet, disturbance, or pest attack. Bulbs should be lifted, cleaned around their base, and replanted in a fresh well drained site. If leaves change from healthy green to an anaemic yellowy shade the bulb is probably an acid lover becoming chlorotic due to the presence of lime. The soil needs the addition of plenty of humus in the form of peat and will be helped by a dusting of sulphur and sulphate of ammonia. It takes considerable amounts of peat to make a marked difference in the pH levels. Be generous. More immediate relief will be afforded by spraying the foliage with a commercial chelated iron compound at the recommended strength.

Leaves eaten. Due to work of adult or larvae of lily beetle.

Flowers distorted. Due to virus or a heavy infestation of aphid.

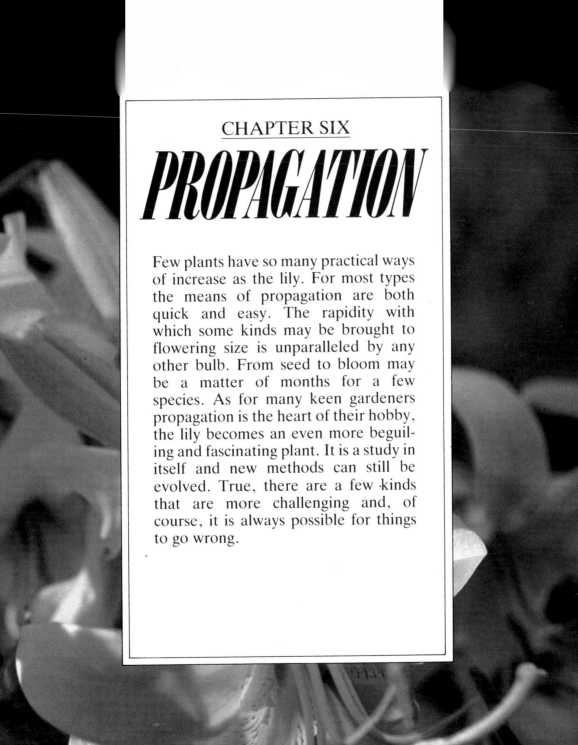

CHAPTER SIX

PROPAGATION

Few plants have so many practical ways of increase as the lily. For most types the means of propagation are both quick and easy. The rapidity with which some kinds may be brought to flowering size is unparalleled by any other bulb. From seed to bloom may be a matter of months for a few species. As for many keen gardeners propagation is the heart of their hobby, the lily becomes an even more beguiling and fascinating plant. It is a study in itself and new methods can still be evolved. True, there are a few kinds that are more challenging and, of course, it is always possible for things to go wrong.

Diagnosis of causes of any failure is likely to point to one or other fairly obvious matter having been overlooked or disregarded. If you have not tried any of the following methods you ought to have a go as few things are more rewarding than fostering the increase of some of your favourite kinds. If you find you have too many bulbs, you will certainly find you have plenty of interested friends ready to accept a gift.

Choices of methods are:

1. Division of the bulbs;
2. Growing from seed;
3. Growing on stem bulbils;
4. Harvesting the crop of bulblets produced on the stems below ground;
5. Induction of bulbils from broken off scales.

Virused plants that are important may be cleared of the disease and increased rapidly by micropropagation techniques in laboratories, but this is normally a rather expensive professional resource and not one for the amateur.

BULB DIVISION

This would seem to be the most obvious method of increasing stock. It will not give the most dramatic increase but is simple and may be done as part of routine maintenance. In many gardens steady increase of reasonable sized bulbs of particular favourites is likely to be more relevant than the mass production of many small bulbs to be grown on. Division may apply to most types and if done at the correct time should not upset the life cycle of the bulbs. If

you have some rather difficult lilies which seem happy, it could be politic to leave well alone.

The best time to operate is a few weeks after flowering. Flowerheads will have been cut away to prevent seeding and to tidy up. Two or three weeks later the stems may look a little less lively. One digs the bulbs up as carefully as the first root of new potatoes. The main bulbs are easily found and lifted but there may be a number of small bulblets clinging to the stem underground and there may also be a number of small bulbs nestling around the main bulbs. All this small fry can be grown on for a season and will probably then provide flowering bulbs so this bounty should not be scorned.

The obvious difference between lily bulbs and plants like potatoes and bulbs like daffodils is that the lilies are formed of separate scales and in some types these are brittle and will break off distressingly easily if not handled with care.

Where bulbs are growing well it is normal for new bulbs to have formed each side of the flower stem. After one year a single bulb may become two, three, or four new ones if well grown. This would be the pattern with bulbs such as the Asiatic Hybrids. Others could be steadier. How often to lift is a question that worries some. Best to leave well alone and wait to lift any clump until it is becoming crowded. Bulbs will benefit then from being given more room and fresh soil. Whilst it may be possible to gently separate the lifted bulbs by hand, there may be some that look ready to separate but are still joined and these may be cut apart by using a sharp strong knife. Cut surfaces should be treated with fungicide.

Divided bulbs should be replanted immediately in their fresh site in well dug soil with added fertilizer just like newly purchased stock. Having been planted they may be given a good soak. Roots should be preserved and carefully spread around when planting. Some will remain active at least until a fresh crop grow to take over the main duties.

Some American species and hybrids like *L.pardalinum* and its derivatives do not produce separate bulbs below ground but a mat of tough stems furnished with stubby scales. Growing points on these mats can be distinguished and show where new flowering stems are going to be produced the following season. Such matted rootstocks need to be lifted with great care or you will be left with a confetti litter of broken scales. Each growing point with a section of old rootstock can be severed from the parent plant using a strong knife and replanted like a normal bulb.

As with any form of vegetative propagation care should be taken to ensure that the parent material is free of disease. To have one virused bulb is bad enough, to start increasing their number could be disastrous.

SEED

One immediate advantage of raising bulbs from seed is that the new plants start life clear of any disease. Seed is normally produced freely: a pod is capable of giving dozens of seeds, perhaps over a hundred. The resulting plants of seed collected from species are going to be more or less replicas of the parent, but there is always a chance of some improvement in flower form or colour, and it is possible that, by selection, strains can be raised of improved vigour. Seed saved from cultivars, being of mixed genetic make-up, is going to produce a range of different plants, some of which may be as good as, or better, or worse than the parents. It may well be worth trying some for the fun of seeing what comes: you may be the raiser of some new winning kind.

To ensure seed it is best to pollinate a flower or two oneself. Taking hold of an anther with tweezers, pollen may be dusted all over the stigma of the flower. When the petals fall the pods begin to develop. It is soon obvious which ones are going to produce seed; they become fatter and maintain a healthy colour. Most amateurs will only need one pod of seed of the type they want to increase or hybridize. All other pods should be cut away and the chosen pod given every encouragement to ripen early. For this reason it will gain a few days by pollinating the first flower out. The pod and plant are best sprayed with a systemic fungicide. This avoids the pods being attacked by fungus which, once it has penetrated the pod, will send out its mycelium through the maturing seeds and render them all useless.

All will normally be perfectly straightforward with the earlier flowering kinds. Some later ones may be more difficult as there is not all that amount of good

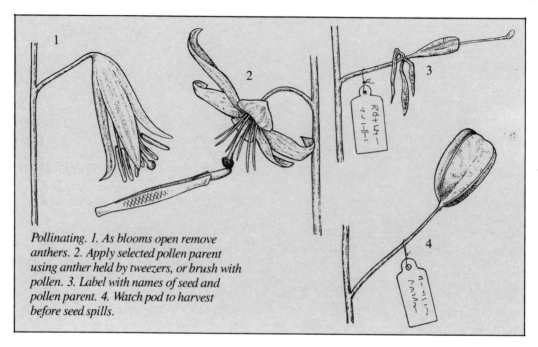

Pollinating. 1. As blooms open remove anthers. 2. Apply selected pollen parent using anther held by tweezers, or brush with pollen. 3. Label with names of seed and pollen parent. 4. Watch pod to harvest before seed spills.

ripening weather after flowering. You may have to harvest your pods and attempt to finish the ripening process under glass in the greenhouse or conservatory. If this has to be resorted to, cut the pod with a foot or more of stem and hang the whole from a spot where the stem is in a dry airy position, preferably getting the benefit of what sun there may be. Precautions against fungus disease are even more important with late harvested pods.

Pods split from the top when ripe. In the wild the flat light seeds are blown away. We shall be watching for this stage and can then harvest the pods and lay them on a sheet of paper to be opened and shaken free, or to do their last bit of ripening. Cleanliness or protection from fungus is essential.

Seed may be sown immediately after being harvested or kept to be sown in late winter or early spring. Behaviour of seeds varies. Some germinate straight away, some kinds wait for a period. Some germinate and send up a cotyledon leaf to signal the beginning of the process. Other types germinate by sending a shoot downwards, forming the beginnings of a bulb and then later produce their first true leaf above ground. Unless you know precisely how your seed is likely to behave it is a mistake to assume that nothing is happening because of a lack of activity above ground.

The following is a rough and ready guide to how the seeds of different lilies behave. Above ground means that the seed germinates and sends up a leaf into

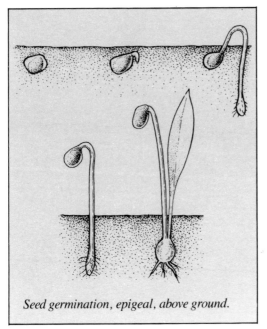

Seed germination, epigeal, above ground.

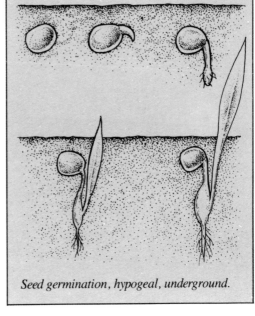

Seed germination, hypogeal, underground.

the air, probably only a little strap-like effort and sometimes still holding the seed case on its tip.

Above ground, without delay:
Asiatic species: _L. cernuum, concolor, davidii, lancifolium, pumilum, nepalense_
Trumpet species: _L. formosanum, longiflorum, regale_
Asiatic and Trumpet Hybrids

Below ground, without delay:
L. dauricum

Above ground, with delay:
L. candidum, henryi, pyrenaicum

Below ground, with delay:
Oriental species: _L. auratum, speciosum_
Candidum group species: _L. candidum,_ _monadelphum, szovitsianum_
American species: _L. canadense, michiganense, pardalinum, superbum_
Martagon species: _L. hansonii, martagon_
Oriental, American group, Martagon Hybrids.

As a general rule the sooner the seed is sown the better. However, if it is harvested very late, say early autumn onwards, it is probably best kept and sown in late winter or early spring. It should be dusted with fungicide, dried, and kept in a cool airy spot. The seeds of those that germinate below ground with a delay, require a period of 12 weeks' warmth, around 21°C (70°F), before at least a four-week period of cold, around 4°C (40°F). The warmth stimulates the formation of bulbs, the cold triggers the metabolism of the bulbs into producing leaves. A natural instance would be the seed of *L. martagon* falling to the ground in the summer to enjoy a period of warmth before the winter sets in to provide somewhat more than four weeks' cool. The little bulbs get under way again in the warmer spring weather.

Seed that germinates without any delay above or below ground can be sown immediately on ripening if harvested early. The young plants have a chance of producing a reasonable small bulb before the winter. Over winter they should be kept out of frost. The following season they may be grown strongly once started, giving plenty of water and feed as they develop. Obviously drainage needs to be good.

I would favour a seed compost made up of equal volumes of good sterilized loam, coarse peat and grit or similar inert material. The containers may be pots, boxes, or simply beds made up in the cool greenhouse or in frames. Seed is best dusted or made wet with fungicide before sowing. Seeds should be sown clear of each other and covered with a light covering of compost. They should be kept moist at all times.

After a season's growth the seedlings can be pricked out into fresh containers, frames or in the open ground. Their new compost should be an open mix with plenty of humus and good drainage. If the pricking out is done at the end of the summer the plants have a chance to get a roothold before the winter. They should be protected from frost in this first winter. Under cover the atmo-

sphere for the growing plants should be buoyant and airy; a still stagnant one is going to provide fertile ground for fungus troubles. It is as well to spray with fungicide in the early stages.

Seed sown in late winter of *L. longiflorum* or *L. formosanum* and grown well could be flowering by the autumn. *L. regale* may be had at flowering stage in 18 months. Some Asiatic Hybrids can be brought to blooming in their second season with care. Even adding an extra season, this rate of development is still quick for bulbs. To sober us up, getting flowering bulbs of *L. martagon* is a long job: it may take from four to seven years from seed.

STEM BULBILS

Species like *L. lancifolium* and hybrids like 'Festival' make the most fecund rabbit blush with shame. Every leaf axil will have at least one bulbil, dark, fat, looking like a miniature bulb and ready to get into fast growing order. Some will have the first little leaf poking up. The technique is simplicity itself. One gathers all the bulbils as they begin to become ripe and are easily dislodged from their perch. You could sit in a deckchair and leave it to the children to do. Having got all the harvest safely gathered in, the bulbils can be 'sown' like seeds in drills and covered by 3–5cm (1–2in) of soil, perhaps in the vegetable garden. They can be left there in the open undisturbed for a season. They will immediately start to root and produce leaf. The plan is to get the little plants well established before the winter when they can be kept free of slugs and frost and be ready to burst into activity with the spring. You can also place the bulbils in pots or boxes of compost and grow them on under cover. With care this will ensure more certainly that you have substantial little bulbs before the winter arrives again. It will make it easier to keep them free of frost. In the spring they can be planted out and grown on outside.

Quite a number of the Asiatic Hybrids will produce bulbils of their own volition, especially those showing some *L. lancifolium* ancestry. However many others can be encouraged to give bounteous crops by a little judicious management. Most gardeners are likely to get more than they need from one stem of bulbils. Therefore the sacrifice of one flowering stem may be thought a price well worth paying. What needs doing is to sever neatly the complete flowering head as soon as this can be seen, leaving the remainder of the stem undamaged. 'Enchantment' and all others of this persuasion will react strongly to this decapitation. The energy that would have gone into the flower production would seem to be diverted into the growing of large quantities of bulbils. Most leaf axils will have at least one and, as there are plenty of leaves on most of these stems, one is talking about a lot of bulbils. Sometimes the lesser stems seem to be even more prolific than the larger ones so you may not be sacrificing that many flowers to get your crop.

Again it is worth emphasizing that only the obviously healthy stems should

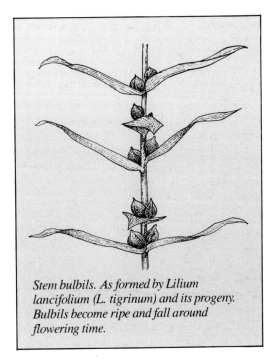

Stem bulbils. As formed by Lilium lancifolium (L. tigrinum) and its progeny. Bulbils become ripe and fall around flowering time.

be used for propagation. Strong bulbils can certainly be brought into bloom in their second season if looked after and grown well. *L. lancifolium* can be blooming the year after planting the bulbils, and the strong growing Asiatics are similarly quick.

Bulbils may be encouraged to grow as fast as possible under glass in a well aerated compost and fed half strength tomato fertilizer as soon as a reasonable root system is operating.

BULBLETS BELOW GROUND

Many lilies will produce bulblets on the stems below ground. Whilst most bulbs send their flowering stems direct from

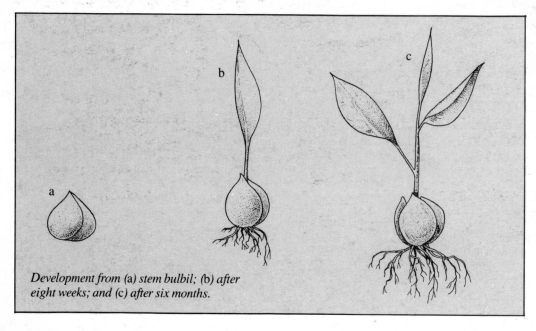

*Development from (a) stem bulbil; (b) after
eight weeks; and (c) after six months.*

the bulb to the nearest airspace, there
are a few devious characters that allow
their stems to wander around below the
ground before ascending into daylight.
The upright stems of Asiatic and some
other types will often produce numbers
of bulblets on the stems often close to
where the stems are rooting.

The stems may be induced to produce
more bulblets by being earthed up with
good humus-rich compost for several
inches a little while before flowering.
Indeed quite soon after flowering the
stem can be pulled out of the bulb or the
bulb lifted carefully and the stem cut
through close to the bulb. These stems
are then replanted separately and kept
moist so that the goodness of the stem
eventually goes into the enlargement of
the bulblets rather than into the further
fattening of the parent bulb. The stem

*Opposite: 'Stargazer' is an Oriental Hybrid
which blooms freely from small bulbs.*

bulblets can range from quite sizeable
offerings to very small pieces that will
need nurturing to grow eventually into
reasonable plants. These bulblets can be
harvested some time after flowering, say
about four to six weeks. For most types
this allows plenty of time for the bulblets to get well rooted and become
independent bulbs before the winter.

The limited number of types that have
wandering stoloniferous stems below
ground will produce good sized bulbs at
intervals along these stems. As the new
bulbs are naturally separated it will be
pointless to try to harvest these too
early. It could be that they are best left
alone and only when the group becomes too crowded need the gardener

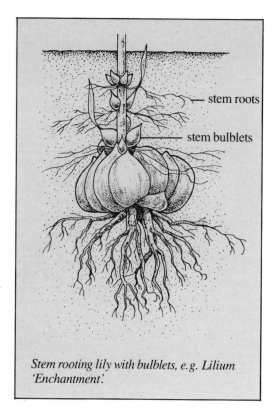

Stem rooting lily with bulblets, e.g. Lilium 'Enchantment'.

— stem roots

— stem bulblets

arrive and effect some wider dispersion in the autumn or at the beginning of the spring.

SCALES

This is a favourite technique, favoured because it is so easy, reliable and enjoyable to do. The first and overriding factor is the selection of healthy bulbs to propagate. There should be no suspicion of virus.

Various procedures may be adopted. The main principles are laid down here. How you apply them will be your choice.

Scales may be taken at any time but the best period will be a short while after flowering or in the early spring. A number of plump scales can be removed from the outside and the parent bulb planted without it suffering unduly. Half dead scales are going to be useless. Whether a bulb has been lifted after flowering, or a bulb used in the spring before planting, the broken surfaces of the main bulb and the scales should be treated with fungicide. Bulbs and scales should be planted as soon as possible.

Scales require moisture, air and warmth. How one supplies these matters little. The temperature should be around 21°C (70°F). A temperature of not less than 15°C (60°F) is really advisable. Moisture should be constant without drenching the scales; wet conditions will be likely to result in rotting and failure. Air is important. One possibility is to place the scales in a plastic bag or glass jar of damp vermiculite with a very light dusting of fungicide for safety's sake. Having carefully labelled these containers inside and out, they may be placed somewhere to enjoy constant heat. They do not need light and so could be placed in the airing cupboard or near the central heating boiler or even on a kitchen shelf: in fact anywhere that you can prove to yourself the temperature is more or less constant at the recommended levels.

More usually scales are lined out in trays of compost. The top third of each scale may be left protruding and provides a useful handle when dealing with the scales later. Alternatively the whole scale can be covered. Compost can be of

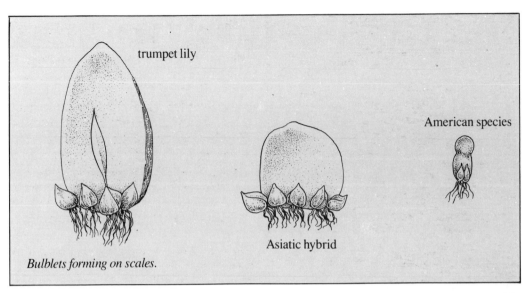

trumpet lily

American species

Asiatic hybrid

Bulblets forming on scales.

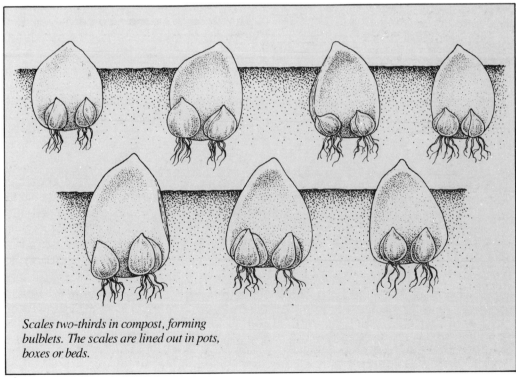

Scales two-thirds in compost, forming bulblets. The scales are lined out in pots, boxes or beds.

Above: *Lilies of the upward-facing L. ×
hollandicum types in an early summer border.*

Opposite: *A dark evergreen hedge makes an
ideal backcloth for light coloured lilies.*

equal parts of coarse peat and perlite, grit, or really coarse clean sand. I find perlite the best, it is inert and uniform. Having got all the scales in and labelled, the tray can be watered, allowed to drain and then enclosed in a polythene bag with plenty of air. Placed in the greenhouse or conservatory at the temperature recommended, they will need little attention apart from an occasional glance until the bulbils have formed.

Even this may be more elaborate than is necessary. Scales could be laid on a piece of capillary matting on the greenhouse bench, covered with moss or dampened course peat and covered with plastic. All will go well.

From one to perhaps four bulbils should have formed after about five weeks and then the scales can be carefully removed and potted up in growing compost either in individual pots or trays, or lined out in frames or even outside in a drill. If planted outside they will need soil that is conducive to rapid healthy growth. By the end of the growing season plants of reasonable size should have resulted. In two seasons they may all be flowering, *L. martagon*, however, may take twice as long. As there always seems to be a shortage of all the *L.martagon* types it makes sense to have a propagation scheme in hand as soon as possible.

There are a few points that may be borne in mind as one grows batches of lilies from small plants. They grow quickly and the aim should be to keep them growing without check. This means that they need plenty of water whilst growing, but the lily is not a plant that likes being drowned, therefore the drainage should be first rate. As plants grow so strongly, if they are initially planted closely they are going to finish at the end of the season being far too crowded. It is sensible to give the young plants plenty of room. They need air around them. If they get too thick they will stand considerable risk of becoming drawn, soft and liable to collapse or fungus attack. Regular spraying with fungicide will make good sense. A watch should be kept for aphids as they attack even the smallest plants.

RECOMMENDATIONS

Particularly quick results by growing from seed may be obtained from the species *L. longiflorum, philippinense, formosanum, f. pricei, regale, pumilum,* and *concolor*. The first four can grow big enough to bloom within twelve months of sowing. The last three may flower in their second year if grown well, otherwise they should be full size by their third season. Amongst the hybrids, the Asiatic hybrids and the trumpets are the quickest. *L. martagon* may take six years to bloom from seed!

Scales provide an equally fast route to flowering plants for those species listed quick from seed. Scales are normally a more certain and quicker way for species like *L. martagon, monadelphum, szovitsianum, speciosum* and *auratum*. It is particularly important to ensure that the last two are clear of virus as they are very much more liable to such troubles than most.

I have had very good results from scales of *L. martagon* and its hybrids with *L. hansonii* when grown in the open where the scales have been detached after flowering, lined out in well drained soil, and completely covered. Such scales need to be treated with fungicide before planting and the site kept clean of weeds. The site should remain undisturbed for a couple of seasons, above ground there may be no sign of activity the first year.

Those kinds that naturally produce bulbils in their leaf axils, or that can be induced to do so by early decapitation of their flower heads, may be encouraged to reach their maximum rate of increase in the following manner. Scales are removed and planted as recommended in the early summer and planted under glass or polythene. The resulting plants are grown strongly and lined out early the next year in boxes or greenhouse beds. They are grown strongly to produce stems. The stems of these small bulbs give a proportionately much larger harvest of bulbils than mature bulbs. Bulbils can be harvested early and grown on to produce further small bulbs to be similarly treated. Removing any precocious bloom will divert the energy to bulbil production.

All the Asiatic hybrids with *L. bulbiferum* or *L. lancifolium* (*L. tigrinum*) in their ancestry can probably be made to produce plenty of bulbils by decapitation even if, in normal growth, they never or only rarely do so. Again it is important to emphasize that one must make sure that only healthy plants are used to start any such vegetative method of increase.

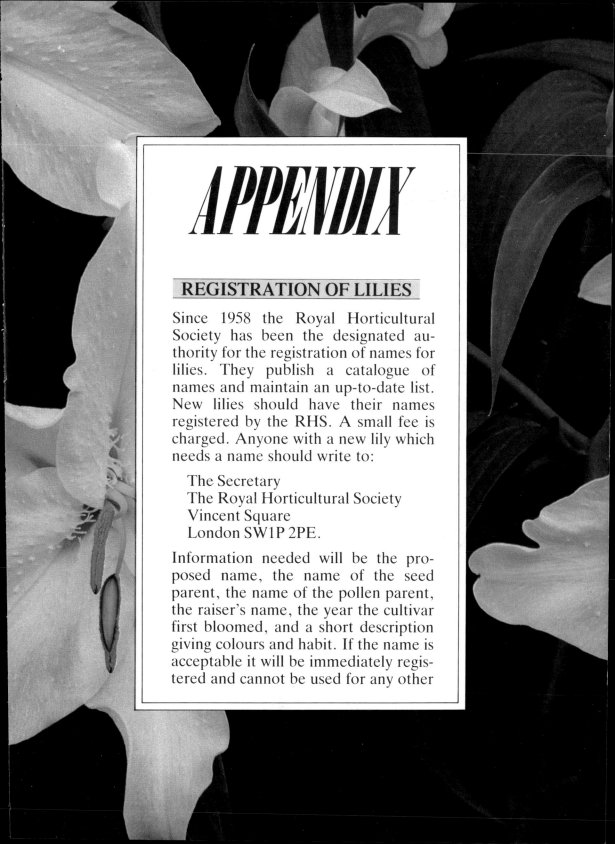

APPENDIX

REGISTRATION OF LILIES

Since 1958 the Royal Horticultural Society has been the designated authority for the registration of names for lilies. They publish a catalogue of names and maintain an up-to-date list. New lilies should have their names registered by the RHS. A small fee is charged. Anyone with a new lily which needs a name should write to:

The Secretary
The Royal Horticultural Society
Vincent Square
London SW1P 2PE.

Information needed will be the proposed name, the name of the seed parent, the name of the pollen parent, the raiser's name, the year the cultivar first bloomed, and a short description giving colours and habit. If the name is acceptable it will be immediately registered and cannot be used for any other kind, nor can a name that is likely to be confused with the chosen one. It is sometimes worth sending an alternative name for fear the first one should be unacceptable or already taken.

RHS LILY GROUP

Membership of this group costs a very modest fee. For this you can enjoy the following benefits. A newsletter is published and visits to various gardens featuring lilies are arranged. Lectures take place. A show of lilies from members of the group is arranged in conjunction with one of the RHS shows in July. The group produces an annual yearbook crammed with lily lore and news. At one of the RHS autumn shows the group holds its AGM and following this an auction of bulbs donated by members is held. This is a very useful and entertaining occasion when it is possible to buy bulbs of unusual kinds and ones that you may be as sure as anything is in this world that the stock is clean. The Membership Secretary can be contacted through the RHS.

Members of the group are encouraged to save seed of both their species and hybrids. This is donated to a central pool so that all members may then have the chance of packets from a very diverse list. For anyone with a more than very casual interest in lilies this seed exchange can be the most likely source of interesting and unusual forms. This facility alone is worth many times the modest group membership fee.

LILY SOCIETIES

Britain lacks a society devoted to lilies. This is in a sense a compliment to the RHS Lily Group. It really undertakes the work of a separate society under the aegis of the RHS and does this economically. Abroad there are flourishing societies in the USA, in Holland and New Zealand. Current addresses of these may be obtained from the RHS.

The North American Lily Society is particularly lively. It supports the cultivation of lilies in many ways but especially by up-to-date interesting publications, by giving awards to outstanding new cultivars, encouraging shows, and providing a panel of judges. A wealth of advice is available on all aspects of lily culture in the various climatic zones of the USA. Enthusiasts outside the USA can join to take advantage of the stimulating society literature. There are also locally orientated lily organizations in the USA.

LILY GARDENS

In different parts of the country there are gardens with collections of lilies. Local knowledge will be valuable as collections change. One can expect to find some at any of the botanical gardens such as Kew, Edinburgh, Oxford, and Cambridge. There are good lots to be seen in the RHS Garden at Wisley, at the Savill Garden, Windsor, and at Harlow Car, the gardens of the Northern Horticultural Society near Harrogate.

BIBLIOGRAPHY

This is a short bibliography of lily literature that may be helpful for those wishing to read more widely.

A Monograph of the Genus Lilium, Elwes, London, 1880.

A rare botanical treatise with hand painted illustrations which may have to be consulted in a specialist library, such as the R.H.S. Lindley library.

A Supplement to Elwes's Monograph, Grove and Cotton, London, 1934-40.

With hand painted illustrations by Lilian Snelling.

The Lilies of Eastern Asia, a Monograph, E. H. Wilson, London, 1925.

A valuable account by the explorer and collector who knew more about lilies in these habitats than anyone at that time.

The Lily Year Books, R.H.S., from 1933 onwards.

Full of information about the current state of lilies in cultivation.

A Book of Lilies, Stoker, Penguin, 1945.

A charming small book in the King Penguin series.

Lilies of the World, Woodcock and Stearn, Country Life Ltd., 1950.

A treatise dealing mainly with the species in a thorough botanical way but with full notes on cultivation. Not written in a frightening style.

Modern Lilies, M. Jefferson-Brown, Faber, 1965.

Covers species and main hybrids of the period.

Lilies. Jan de Graaff and Edward Hyams, Nelson, 1967.

General book but gives a good account of the Jan de Graaff hybridisation programme.

Lilies. P. Synge, Batsford, 1980.

The most complete up-to-date botanical treatise of the genus.

Growing Lilies, Derek Fox, Croom Helm, 1985.

Interesting account by the grower and raiser of many fine lilies.

Lilies, Derek Fox, Cassell/R.H.S., 1985.

Handy paperback introduction to lilies in the 'Wisley Handbook' series.

Lilies of China, Stephen Haw, Batsford, 1986.

Authoritative account of the lilies from this, the homeland of most wild lilies.

The Lily, M. Jefferson-Brown, David and Charles, 1988.

192 pages covering most aspects. Reviews species and hybrids most likely to be found in gardens or in gardening literature.

A group of regal lilies forms an eye-catching feature in a mixed border which includes the grass, Helictotrichon sempervirens and silver-leaved artemisia.

INDEX

ACKNOWLEDGEMENTS

The publishers gratefully acknowledge the following agencies/photographers for granting permission to reproduce the following colour photographs: Michael Jefferson-Brown (pp. 17, 24, 44, 49 (upper), 52, 60, 68 (upper), 69 (both), 72, 76/77, 81, 84, 85, 89, 96, 97 & 113); Harry Smith Horticultural Photographic Collection (pp. 8/9, 13, 29, 33, 48, 49 (lower), 68 (lower), 73, 101, 104/105 & 124); Tania Midgley (pp. 20/21 & 100); Pat Brindley (pp. 41 & 64); Photos Horticultural Picture Library (pp. 45, 53, 56/57, 65, 93 & 120/121); and Images Colour Library (p. 117).

All the line drawings are by Nils Solberg.